ISEE Middle Level Practice Tests

ISEE Middle Level Practice Tests

Three Full-Length Verbal and Quantitative
Mock Tests with Detailed Answer Explanations

ANTHEM PRESS

Anthem Press
An imprint of Wimbledon Publishing Company
www.anthempress.com

This edition first published in UK and USA 2023
by ANTHEM PRESS
75–76 Blackfriars Road, London SE1 8HA, UK
or PO Box 9779, London SW19 7ZG, UK
and
244 Madison Ave #116, New York, NY 10016, USA

© Accel Learning LLC www.accellearning.com 2023

ISEE is not involved in the publication of this book and does not
endorse or sponsor this work.

British Library Cataloguing-in-Publication Data
A catalogue record for this book is available from the British Library.

Library of Congress Control Number: 2023936662
A catalog record for this book has been requested.

ISBN-13: 978-1-83998-983-4 (Pbk)
ISBN-10: 1-83998-983-1 (Pbk)

This title is also available as an e-book.

Contents

ISEE Overview

About ISEE

What is the ISEE?

What is ISEE? The Independent School Entrance Examination (ISEE) is an exam created and administered by the Educational Records Bureau (ERB). It tests students' individual academic achievements and reasoning skills as a basis for admission to private schools in the United States and internationally. The ISEE is the admission test of choice for many independent schools throughout the country and abroad.

The ISEE has five sections (in order of testing): Verbal Reasoning, Quantitative Reasoning, Reading Comprehension and Vocabulary, Mathematics Achievement, and an Essay which is written by the student in response to a given writing prompt. Each section is designed to tap into a unique aspect of a student's preparation for academic work. The first four sections consist entirely of multiple-choice questions.

How does a student arrange to take the ISEE?

Students may take the ISEE in one of the following ways:

1. The ISEE is given at individual school test sites at a wide variety of schools throughout the country and abroad and on a number of test dates.

2. The ISEE can also be given at the ERB office in New York and at offices in other parts of the country, visit: www.erblearn.org for more details.

What types of Questions are on the ISEE?

The first four sections are composed of multiple-choice questions. The fifth section, the essay, is not scored but requires the student to respond to a preselected writing prompt.

The first two sections, **Verbal Reasoning** and **Quantitative Reasoning**, measure the applicant's reasoning ability.

The **Verbal Reasoning** test consists of two types of items: vocabulary and sentence completion.

At the Middle Level, the **Quantitative Reasoning** test consists of word problems.

The next two sections, **Reading Comprehension and Vocabulary** and **Mathematics Achievement**, measure the applicant's ability to correctly answer curriculum-based concepts that are appropriate at that grade level.

In order to determine a student's **reading comprehension** skills, in the Reading Comprehension and Vocabulary section, the student is asked to read a passage and then answer items specific to that passage.

Mathematics Achievement items conform to national mathematics standards and ask the student to identify the problem and find a solution to a problem. The items require one or more steps in calculating the answer.

The **Essay** is written by the student in response to a writing "prompt" or topic that is grade-level appropriate. The prompts rotate throughout the testing season. They are designed to prompt a student to write an informed essay on a particular topic.

The table below gives a quick snapshot of the questions in the ISEE.

Test Section	Questions	Time	Details
Verbal Reasoning	40–34	20 minutes	Tests vocabulary and reasoning abilities Synonym section focuses on word recognition Sentence Completion section measures students' knowledge of words and their function Use context clues to decide which word best fits the sentence
Quantitative Reasoning	38–37	35 minutes	Tests mathematical synthesis, skill, comprehension, and logical reasoning Quantitative Reasoning problems are higher-order thinking problems Interpreting data Solving application problems Estimating Recognizing patterns Solving nonroutine problems
Reading Comprehension and Vocabulary	36–25	35–25 minutes	Tests reading ability through six to eight passages, depending on the ISEE test level Each passage is followed by at least four text-related questions
Mathematics Achievement	47–30	40–30 minutes	Correlates with common mathematics curriculum taught in schools Students may NOT use calculators on the ISEE
Essay	1	30 minutes	Students' essays must be in response to a provided prompt Students' essays are sent to each school that receives the ISEE score report Essays are NOT SCORED, but are instead evaluated individually by each school The ISEE essay section is intended for students to demonstrate their writing abilities

How will this book help me?

This book is structured just like the real ISEE. As you practice the tests given in this book, it will help you with:

- Build confidence.
- Get clarity on the topics.
- Build knowledge about the ISEE.
- Understand your strengths and weaknesses.
- Become familiar with the test layout, structure, and level of difficulty.

ISEE Test Taking

Why should one take the ISEE?

The school you are applying to has requested ISEE scores as part of the overall admissions process. By requiring an admission test for all students entering the same grade, the school can view one common item of all applicants. The school looks at many items in conjunction with the ISEE scores, including your application, your current school records, and possibly an interview. All components of the admission process, including the ISEE scores, help the school, you, and your family determine the best school match for you.

How many times can I take the ISEE?

The ISEE may be taken only when making a formal application to a school(s). You may take the ISEE only once per admission season, and you may not take the ISEE for practice.

What can I expect at the test site on the day of the test?

Students will present their verification letter or identification to be checked in upon arrival. They will be directed to the testing room. They will be provided with the testing material and other supplies. Although test administrators may not discuss test questions during the test, they give clear test directions, and you are encouraged to ask for clarification, if necessary, before beginning each section of the test.

Are there any scheduled breaks during the test?

There are two breaks—one following the Quantitative Reasoning section and another following the Math Achievement section. Each break is 5 minutes long.

What materials do I need to bring to the actual ISEE?

Students should bring four #2 pencils and two pens with either blue or black ink. Students may choose to use erasable ink.

Are there materials that are prohibited from using during the ISEE?

Scrap paper, calculators, smart watches, rulers, protractors, compasses, dictionaries, and cellphones are NOT permitted during the actual test.

Is there penalty for a wrong answer? Can I guess?

There is no penalty for a wrong answer, but it is not advised to guess.

ISEE Results

What happens to my scores?

After you take the ISEE and your answer sheet is scored, ERB will send copies of the scores and the essay you wrote to the schools that you have chosen, within 7–10 business days. They will send a copy of your test scores (but not a copy of the essay) to your family.

How is the essay scored?

The essay is not scored. However, a copy is sent to the school(s) to which a student sends score reports as indicated on the registration. Evaluation is based on each individual school's criteria.

How soon will I receive my scores?

Students will receive the scores in 7–10 business days.

What is the raw score?

A raw score represents the number correct. If a student got 35 items correct—say on a test of 40 questions—then the raw score is simply 35.

What is the scaled score?

Scaled score is a raw score that has been converted to a different numerical scale, e.g., 200–800. The raw score scale ranges from 0 to maximum score, while the scaled score range consists of higher numbers with a somewhat arbitrary minimum and maximum score. The range of scaled scores on the ISEE is 760–940.

What is the percentile score?

A percentile score is a relative score compared to other independent school applicants who have applied to the same grade during the past three years.

The percentile ranking helps private schools compare a student's performance with others in their applicant cohorts. **The higher your percentile, the better your ISEE score.** For example, a 45th percentile ranking means that the student scored the same as or better than 45% of students in the last three years.

What is a stanine?

A stanine score is simply another scale and is based on percentile ranks. Percentile ranks range from 1 to 99, while stanines range from 1 to 9. In general, a stanine score of 1–3 is below average, 4–6 is average, and 7–9 is above average.

How will I know if I passed or failed?

Students do not pass or fail the ISEE. There is no cutoff point that determines pass/fail status or divides students into these two groups. There is no cutoff (or pass/fail) score recommended by ERB.

ISEE—Middle Level Exam-1

Introduction

The **Independent School Entrance Exam (ISEE Exam)** is a school entrance exam taken by students in grades 4–12 seeking admission into private schools and non-Catholic religious schools throughout the United States. The Middle Level ISEE Exam is for students currently in grades 6 and 7 who are candidates for admission to grades 7 and 8.

The ISEE is an admission test that has three levels: A Lower Level, Middle Level, and Upper Level. The Lower Level is for students currently in grades 4 and 5 who are candidates for admission to grades 5 and 6. The Middle Level is for students in grades 6 and 7 who are candidates for grades 7 and 8. The Upper Level is for students in grades 8–11 who are candidates for grades 9–12.

Summary

Who can take the test?	Students from grades 6 and 7			
When is the test conducted?	Students may register to take the ISEE one time in any or all of three testing seasons. The ISEE testing seasons are defined as Fall (August–November), Winter (December–March), and Spring/Summer (April–July)			
What is the format of the test?	All questions are multiple choice			
What is the medium of the test?	Paper based			
What are the topics covered in the test?	**Test Section**	**Questions**	**Time**	**Details**
	Verbal Reasoning	40–34	20 minutes	Tests vocabulary and reasoning abilities Synonym section focuses on word recognition Sentence Completion section measures students' knowledge of words and their function Use context clues to decide which word best fits the sentence
	Quantitative Reasoning	38–37	35 minutes	Tests mathematical synthesis, skill, comprehension, and logical reasoning Quantitative Reasoning problems are higher-order thinking problems Interpreting data Solving application problems Estimating Recognizing patterns Solving nonroutine problems
	Reading Comprehension and Vocabulary	36–25	35–25 minutes	Tests reading ability through six to eight passages, depending on the ISEE test level Each passage is followed by at least four text-related questions

(Continued)

(Continued)

	Mathematics Achievement	47–30	40–30 minutes	Correlates with common mathematics curriculum taught in schools Students may NOT use calculators on the ISEE
	Essay	1	30 minutes	Students' essays must be in response to a provided prompt Students' essays are sent to each school that receives the ISEE score report Essays are NOT SCORED, but are instead evaluated individually by each school The ISEE essay section is intended for students to demonstrate their writing abilities
How long is the test?	Depending on the level, the actual testing time is between **2 hours and 20 minutes to 2 hours and 40 minutes.**			

Verbal Reasoning

You have 20 minutes to answer the 40 questions in the Verbal Reasoning Section.

This section is divided into two parts that contain two different types of questions. As soon as you have completed Part I, answer the questions in Part II. You may write in your test booklet. For each answer you select, fill in the corresponding circle on your answer document.

Part I—Synonyms

Each question in Part I consists of a word in capital letters followed by four answer choices. Select the one word that is most nearly the same in meaning as the word in capital letters.

SAMPLE QUESTION:	Sample Answer
CHARGE:	A B ● D
(A) release	
(B) belittle	
(C) accuse	
(D) conspire	

Part II—Sentence Completion

Each question in Part II is made up of a sentence with one blank. Each blank indicates that a word or phrase is missing. The sentence is followed by four answer choices. Select the word or phrase that will best complete the meaning of the sentence as a whole.

SAMPLE QUESTIONS:	Sample Answer
It rained so much that the streets were _____.	● B C D
(A) flooded	
(B) arid	
(C) paved	
(D) crowded	
The house was so dirty that it took _____.	A B C ●
(A) less than 10 min to wash it	
(B) four months to demolish it	
(C) over a week to walk across it	
(D) two days to clean it	

5

Part I—Synonyms

Directions:

Select the word that is most nearly the same in meaning as the word in capital letters.

1. ADJUDICATE

   (A) settle (B) prolong (C) extend (D) sustain

2. ADROIT

   (A) adept (B) clumsy (C) incompetent (D) probationary

3. ANALOGOUS

   (A) opposite (B) parallel (C) unrelated (D) irrelevant

4. ASSIMILATE

   (A) refuse (B) embrace (C) reject (D) defy

5. AVERT

   (A) confront (B) indulge (C) avoid (D) accept

6. BEMOAN

   (A) applaud (B) commend (C) praise (D) deplore

7. BRAZEN

   (A) afraid (B) timid (C) shy (D) bold

8. BRUSQUE

   (A) blunt (B) polite (C) refined (D) discreet

9. CANNY

   (A) foolish (B) reckless (C) sensible (D) careless

10. CAPITULATE

(A) resist (B) surrender (C) withstand (D) oppose

11. DEFUNCT

(A) extant (B) present (C) active (D) obsolete

12. EXPANSE

(A) cage (B) fold (C) extent (D) coop

13. IMPLICIT

(A) tacit (B) explicit (C) direct (D) straight

14. INIMICAL

(A) helpful (B) detrimental (C) advantageous (D) pleasant

15. NOTORIOUS

(A) unknown (B) anonymous (C) infamous (D) incognito

16. MAUL

(A) heal (B) cure (C) mend (D) mangle

17. MORTIFY

(A) indulge (B) horrify (C) satisfy (D) appease

18. PEEVISH

(A) irritable (B) mellow (C) mild (D) amiable

19. REBUKE

(A) praise (B) compliment (C) scold (D) commend

20. REVERBERATE

(A) silent (B) hush (C) shut (D) echo

Part II—Sentence Completion

Directions:

Select the word that best completes the sentence.

21. His mother did not approve of his hobbies because she found them as _____ which will sway his focus.

    (A) boondoggles (B) strategies (C) game plans (D) blueprints

22. A flock of birds flew around the house as if they were giving us a _____ of something terrible coming.

    (A) gift (B) caveat (C) award (D) favor

23. Ian took the opportunity because he saw new hope despite the _____ uncertainties of moving into a new city.

    (A) discreet (B) uncoupled (C) concomitant (D) irrelevant

24. In many cultures, children are _____ to care for their parents when they get older.

    (A) excluded (B) restrained (C) hindered (D) constrained

25. The staff were _____ from walking out the restaurant until the lost money is returned.

    (A) restrained (B) constrained (C) forced (D) allowed

26. It is about time these actions _____ a riot from the townspeople.

    (A) prevent (B) engender (C) restrain (D) dismantle

27. After the city mayor was _____ for corruption, new projects were started under the supervision of the reputable vice mayor.

    (A) acquitted (B) cleared (C) indicted (D) released

28. Carla remained _____ despite her father's persuasion to give up acting.

    (A) compliant (B) flexible (C) passive (D) intransigent

29. Having three children leaves the house in a complete _____ so I can't imagine adding one more.

(A) heaven (B) mayhem (C) peace (D) order

30. You need to _____ a lot of courage if you wish to pursue this path.

(A) disperse (B) muster (C) release (D) leave

31. Her grandfather arranged her to marry this rich man for _____ interests.

(A) noble (B) charitable (C) pecuniary (D) honest

32. We should put our efforts in saving our children from the _____ of our generation's actions.

(A) plight (B) benevolence (C) benefit (D) advantage

33. The mistress' reputation _____ when it became known to the town that she disliked charity.

(A) soared (B) skyrocketed (C) rose (D) plummeted

34. Days went by without water to _____ his thirst.

(A) dry (B) quench (C) intensify (D) amplify

35. Just as when she was at the _____ of her career, a scandal quickly plunged her reputation.

(A) bottom (B) end (C) zenith (D) lowest

36. He jumped with _____ upon seeing his favorite childhood movie on TV.

(A) misery (B) gloom (C) sadness (D) mirth

37. Two little boys _____ him with rotten tomatoes.

(A) pelted (B) awarded (C) honored (D) gifted

38. Damien's arrogance _____ the ladies at court.

(A) smitten (B) attracted (C) perturbed (D) cheered

39. Anna had enough of Lucy's bullying and finally had the courage to _____.

(A) retort (B) exit (C) leave (D) cry

40. The anxious singer _____ at the sight of the big crowd.

(A) smiled (B) laughed (C) triumph (D) winced

End of section.

If you have any time left, go over the questions in this section only.

Do not start the next section.

You have 35 minutes to answer the 37 questions in the Quantitative Reasoning Section.

Each question is followed by four suggested answers. Read each question and then decide which one of the four suggested answers is best.

Find the row of spaces on your document that has the same number as the question. In this row, mark the space having the same letter as the answer you have chosen. You may write in your test booklet.

EXAMPLE 1:   <u>Sample Answer</u>

What is the value of the expression (4 + 6) ÷ 2?   A B ● D

(A) 2
(B) 4
(C) 5
(D) 7

The correct answer is 5, so circle C is darkened.

EXAMPLE 2:

A square has an area of 25 cm². What is the length of one of its side?   A ● C D

(A) 1 cm
(B) 5 cm
(C) 10 cm
(D) 25 cm

The correct answer is 5 cm, so circle B is darkened.

---

1. $68 \times 9 =$

   (A) 216 (B) 356 (C) 612 (D) 572

2. What is the half of the perimeter of a square with a side of 20 ft?

   (A) 40 ft (B) 50 sq. ft (C) 30 ft (D) 80 ft

3. $6 \times 7 \times 14 - (7 \times 7 \times 6 \times 2) =$

   (A) 100 (B) 0 (C) –15 (D) 8

4. Ben scored 88, 85, 95, 60, and 74, respectively, in the examination. How much did he get on average?

   (A) 44.55 (B) 80.40 (C) 90 (D) 89.75

5. What will come in place of question mark (?) in the given questions?
   7 8 18 57 ? 1,165

   (A) 228 (B) 232 (C) 212 (D) 236

6. $\dfrac{63}{9} \div \dfrac{27}{81} =$

   (A) 63 (B) 27 (C) 18 (D) 21

7. If $x = 9$; then find the value of $\dfrac{5x}{5} + 13$

   (A) 13 (B) 9 (C) 22 (D) 26

8. $\sqrt[4]{256} = ?$

   (A) 128 (B) 85 (C) 4 (D) 2

9. $151.04 - 118.95 \div 17.01 - x^2 = 80.07$; find the value of x.

   (A) 6.849 (B) 12.556 (C) 7.9987 (D) 23

10. What is the largest value among these: $\dfrac{3}{8}, \dfrac{1}{4}, \dfrac{5}{6}, \dfrac{3}{10}$

    (A) $\dfrac{3}{8}$ (B) $\dfrac{1}{4}$ (C) $\dfrac{5}{6}$ (D) $\dfrac{3}{10}$

Questions 11–15

Study the table carefully and answer the given questions.

Date regarding number of events booked/held at five different halls in 2016.

Halls	Number of Events Booked	Number of Events Cancelled	Out of Events Held, Percentage of Marriage Receptions
A	242	32	80%
B	254	30	75%
C	210	35	80%
D	280	55	80%
E	265	25	85%
Note: Number of events held = Number of events booked – number of events cancelled.			

11. What was the respected ratio between number of events held at Hall C and those held at Hall D?

    (A) 3:5   (B) 5:7   (C) 3:4   (D) 7:9   (E) 2:3

12. The number of events that were not marriage receptions at Hall E was what percent less than the number of events that were not marriage receptions at Hall A?

    (A) $57\frac{1}{7}\%$ (B) $48\frac{1}{7}\%$ (C) $14\frac{2}{7}\%$ (D) $66\frac{2}{3}\%$

13. At the Hall B in 2018, if number of events held was $1\frac{1}{8}$ times that in 2016 and number of events cancelled increased by 20% over that in 2016, how many events were booked?

    (A) 282   (B) 278   (C) 284   (D) 288

14. What was the average number of marriage receptions held at Halls A, B, and D?

    (A) 162   (B) 172   (C) 156   (D) 148

15. What was the difference between total number of events held at Halls A and E together and those cancelled at the same halls together?

    (A) 393   (B) 383   (C) 403   (D) 398

16. Look at this series 48, 51, 56, 63, …. What number should come next?

    (A) 72   (B) 75   (C) 70   (D) 67

17. $44 \div 0.11 =$

(A) 0.4   (B) 0.04   (C) 400   (D) 40

18. If $3x + 1 = 7$, then what is the value of $20x + x$?

(A) 42   (B) 50   (C) 32   (D) 40

19. $78 \times 78 =$

(A) 2,563   (B) 6,084   (C) 9,985   (D) 5,684

20. What is the value of the digit 8 in the number 9,24,580?

(A) 8   (B) 80   (C) 800   (D) 8,000

Directions:

Using all information given in each question, compare the quantity in Column A to the quantity in Column B. All questions in Part II have these answers choice:

(A) the quantity in Column A is greater

(B) the quantity in Column B is greater

(C) the two quantities are equal

(D) the relationship cannot be determined from the information given

21. 140° x

Column A	Column B
X	40

22. A rectangle with sides x and y has an area of 18.

Column A	Column B
The length of x	The length of y

23.

Column A	Column B
$\sqrt{16} + \sqrt{49}$	$\sqrt{16 + 49}$

24.

The quadrilateral $ABCD$ has an area of 18.

Column A	Column B
The perimeter of $ABCD$	15

25. Martha had $4. She gave half of her money to her sister, Linda. Linda now has $3.

Column A	Column B
The amount of money Martha now has	The amount of money Linda had originally

26. $4x + 11 = 67$

$\frac{y}{3} + 6 = 18$

Column A	Column B
X	y

27.

Column A	Column B
The area of a rectangle with length 7 and width 4	The area of a a square with a side of 5

28. **Number of Cookies Eaten Each Day**

Wednesday	2
Thursday	3
Friday	1
Saturday	2

Column A	Column B
The average number of cookies eaten each day	The number of cookies eaten on Thursday

29.

Column A	Column B
$\sqrt{0.81}$	$\sqrt{8.1}$

30. Amy bought four oranges and seven peaches. The total price of the fruit was $1.50.

Column A	Column B
The cost of one orange	The cost of one peach

31.

Column A	Column B
$-(7)^6$	$(-7)^6$

32. A represents an odd integer greater than 9 and less than 15.
B represents an even integer greater than 9 and less than 15.

Column A	Column B
A × 3	B × 4

33. A 12-sided die with faces numbered 1–12 is rolled.

Column A	Column B
The probability that the result is prime	The probability that the result is odd

34.

Column A	Column B
The fractional part of the figure that is shaded	$\dfrac{3}{20}$

35. Melvin brought a large pizza with 16 slices.

Column A	Column B
The number of slices left if Melvin eats 50% of the pizza	The number of slices left if Melvin eats one-fourth of the pizza

36. The original price of a phone case now on sale was $40.

Column A	Column B
The price of the case after two 20% discount	The price of the case after a single 40% discount

37.	Column A	Column B
	The slope of the line with points (4,2) and (5, 8)	The slope of the line $3x - y = -8$

End of section.

If you have any time left, go over the questions in this section only.

Do not start the next section.

You have 25 minutes to answer the 36 questions in the Reading Comprehension and Vocabulary section.

Directions:

This section contains six short reading passages. Each passage is followed by six questions based on its content. Answer the questions following each passage on the basis of what is stated or implied in that passage. You may write in your test booklet.

Questions 1–6

The value of the U.S. dollar has been on a tear for more than a year against everything from the British pound across the Atlantic to the South Korean won across the Pacific.

After rising again Friday, the dollar is near its highest level in more than two decades against a key index measuring six major currencies, including the euro and Japanese yen. Many professional investors don't expect it to <u>ease off</u> anytime soon.

The dollar's rise affects nearly everyone, even those who will never leave the U.S. borders. Here's a look at what's driving the U.S. dollar higher and what it can mean for investors and households:

WHAT DOES IT MEAN TO SAY THE DOLLAR IS STRONGER?

Essentially that one dollar can buy more of another currency than it could before.

Consider the Japanese yen. A year ago, $1 could get a little less than 110 yen. Now, it can buy 143. That's about 30% more and one of the biggest moves the U.S. dollar has made against another currency.

Foreign currency values are constantly shifting against each other as banks, businesses and traders buy and sell them in time zones around the world.

The U.S. Dollar index, which measures the dollar against the euro, yen and other major currencies, has climbed more than 14% this year. The gain looks even more impressive compared against other investments, most of which have had a dismal year. U.S. stocks are down more than 19%, bitcoin has more than halved and gold has lost more than 7%.

1. The main objective of this passage is

   (A) to explain how the current value of the U.S. dollar affects everyone

   (B) to persuade people to immigrate to the United States

   (C) to convince people not to invest in bitcoin and gold

   (D) to convince people to invest in bitcoin and gold

2. Which currency is higher in value according to the passage?

   (A) U.S. dollar   (B) Japanese yen   (C) South Korean won   (D) none of the above

3. In this passage, how much is 143 Japanese Yen in dollars?

   (A) 110   (B) 1   (C) 13   (D) 30

4. According to the passage, what unit is used to measure the dollar against the euro, yen, and other major currencies?

   (A) stock market   (B) trade   (C) U.S. Dollar index   (D) foreign exchange

5. True or false: The passage enumerated six major currencies used in the key index.

   (A) true   (B) false

6. What does the underlined phrasal verb mean in line 9?

   (A) appear greater   (B) increased in value   (C) amplify interest   (D) become less in degree or intensity

Questions 7–12

A particular kind of poliovirus is spreading in the United States. The U.S. Centers for Disease Control and Prevention has confirmed that the country now joins a list of around 30 other countries where circulation of the virus has been identified. Those countries include the United Kingdom, Israel, Egypt, Yemen and around two dozen in Africa.

The news, announced September 13, comes after the identification in July of a case of paralytic polio in an unvaccinated adult in Rockland County in New York. Public health officials found the case was caused by what's called a vaccine-derived poliovirus (find out more about this kind of poliovirus below). This spurred wastewater surveillance in Rockland and the surrounding counties, because people shed poliovirus in their stool. The wastewater samples showed that the virus was spreading in Rockland and neighboring areas.

In response, New York Governor Kathy Hochul declared a state of emergency on September 9 to expand access to polio vaccination statewide. Three of the counties where poliovirus has been detected in wastewater—Rockland, Orange and Sullivan—have polio vaccination rates of only around 60 percent. The virus has also turned up in New York City and Nassau County.

While most people infected with polio don't have symptoms, some might feel like they have the flu, with fever, fatigue or a sore throat. In rare cases, the virus can cause permanent paralysis, and the disease can turn deadly if that paralysis hits the muscles that control breathing or swallowing. Anyone unvaccinated is at risk of paralytic polio if they get infected.

Widespread vaccination efforts helped eliminate wild polioviruses from the United States in 1979, but public health officials are still working toward eradicating the disease globally (SN: 9/12/19). The new worries about polio in the United States are driven by vaccine-derived versions of the virus spreading in areas with low vaccination.

7. The key point of the passage is

(A) to educate citizens on poliovirus   (B) to prevent people from going to New York

(C) to cause mass panic   (D) to cure poliovirus

8. Which country is not mentioned in the passage where circulation of the virus has been identified?

(A) Vietnam   (B) United Kingdom   (C) Israel   (D) Egypt

9. According to the passage, which county is not part of the poliovirus detection?

(A) Rockland   (B) Orange   (C) Sullivan   (D) Somerset

10. How is poliovirus found in wastewater?

(A) the virus was dumped into sewage by an underground laboratory

(B) the infected people shed poliovirus in their stool

(C) the infected animals drink water from the sewage   (D) not stated in the passage

11. According to the passage, which is not a symptom of polio?

(A) fever   (B) fatigue   (C) toothache   (D) sore throat

12. True or false: According to the passage, it is rare to get permanent paralysis from poliovirus.

(A) true   (B) false

Questions 13–18

Mikoko Pamoja, launched in 2013, is the world's first mangrove-driven carbon credit initiative. It earned the United Nations' Equator Prize in 2017, awarded for innovative solutions to poverty that involve conservation and sustainable use of biodiversity.

Today, mangrove restoration is helping the region enter a new chapter, one where labor and resources are well-managed by local communities instead of being exploited. "The community is now able to run its own affairs," Barua notes. Through innovative solutions and hard work, he says, "we're trying to bring back a semblance of that ecosystem."

The dominant mangrove species in Gazi Forest is *Rhizophora mucronata*. With oval, leathery leaves about the size of a child's palm and spindly branches that reach to the sun, the trees can grow up to 27 meters tall. Their interlaced roots, which grow from the base of the trunk into the salt-water, make these evergreen trees unique.

Salt kills most plants, but mangrove roots separate freshwater from salt for the tree to use. At low tide, the looping roots act like stilts and buttresses, keeping trunks and branches above the waterline and dry. Speckling these roots are thousands of specialized pores, or lenticels. The lenticels open to absorb gases from the atmosphere when exposed, but seal tight at high tide, keeping the mangrove from drowning.

The thickets of roots also prevent soil erosion and buffer coastlines against tropical storms. Within these roots and branches, shorebirds and fish—and in some places, manatees and dolphins—thrive.

Mangrove roots support an ecosystem that stores four times as much carbon as inland forests. That's because the saltwater slows decomposition of organic matter, says Kipkorir Lang'at, a principal scientist at the Kenya Marine and Fisheries Research Institute, or KMFRI. So when mangrove plants and animals die, their carbon gets trapped in thick soils. As long as mangroves stay standing, the carbon stays in the soil.

13. The key point of the passage is

(A) to encourage people to plant mangrove in their community

(B) to educate people how mangrove trees save the environment

(C) to invite people to visit Kenya

(D) to persuade people that it's not a good idea to plant mangrove

14. What initiative was mentioned in the passage which received an award for innovative solutions to poverty that involved conservation and sustainable use of biodiversity?

(A) Gazi   (B) Mikoko Pamoja   (C) *Rhizophora mucronata*   (D) United Nations' Equator Prize

15. Which among the choices below is not a benefit from mangrove trees?

(A) prevents soil erosion   (B) serve as a habitat for shorebirds, fish, manatees, and dolphins

(C) stores four times as much carbon   (D) none of the above

16. As described in the passage, what is a lenticel?

(A) specialized pores   (B) oval, leathery leaves   (C) looping roots   (D) thickets

17. How tall can *Rhizophora mucronata* grow?

(A) 27 cm   (B) 27 m   (C) 27 in   (D) 27 ft

18. In line 36, what does the underlined word mean?

(A) wither   (B) fail   (C) flourish   (D) die

Questions 19–24

Time hasn't made much sense since spring 2020 for many people, myself included. In February 2020, during the Before Times, my family traveled to Barcelona, a relatively carefree trip that now feels like a lifetime ago. Other times, I feel like I blinked, and three years vanished. How can my son be starting fifth grade? He was a second grader just a minute ago.

Welcome to "blursday." Back when the pandemic started, the term hit the zeitgeist. The word captured that sense of time disintegrating as our worlds and routines turned upside down (SN: 9/14/20). Days melted together, then weeks, then years.

As people began wondering about why time felt so <u>out of whack</u>, Simon Grondin, a psychologist at Laval University in Quebec City, and colleagues penned a theory paper seeking to explain the phenomenon. Our time is typically punctuated by events, such as dinner dates or daily commutes, Grondin and his team wrote in October 2020 in *Frontiers in Psychology*. Such events provide temporal landmarks. When those landmarks disappear, days lose their identities. Time loses its definition.

19. The key point of the passage is

(A) to encourage people to go out and make more memories

(B) to stop people from going out so that they don't feel time passing by

(C) to introduce a new word, "blursday"

(D) to explain why time started not making sense since the pandemic started

20. How does the passage describe the new term "blursday"?

(A) between Thursday and Friday   (B) yesterday

(C) that sense of time disintegrating as our worlds and routines turned upside down

(D) any day of the week

21. What does the underlined phrase in line 17 mean?

(A) not in style   (B) out of order   (C) properly aligned   (D) allocated evenly

22. Who wrote the theory explaining the phenomenon when people began wandering why time felt out of order?

    (A) Simon Grondin and colleagues (B) Frontier (C) Psychology (D) The writer of the passage

23. How did Grondin explain the phenomenon of losing track of time in their theory paper?

    (A) time is associated with events, such as dinner dates or daily commutes so when these temporal landmarks disappear, that's when people lose the definition of time

    (B) time is associated with the ticking of the clock and the rise and setting of the sun so when people do not see this, they lose definition of time

    (C) time is relative and people can perceive time however they like (D) not mentioned

24. When was Grondin and his team's theory written in *Frontiers in Psychology*?

    (A) September 2019 (B) October 2021 (C) October 2020 (D) October 2022

Questions 25–30

The likelihood of an extreme epidemic, or one similar to COVID-19, will increase <u>threefold</u> in the coming decades, according to a recent study published in the *Proceedings of the National Academy of Sciences*.

The researchers used data from epidemics from the past 400 years, specifically death rates, length of previous epidemics and the rate of new infectious diseases. Their calculation is a <u>sophisticated</u> prediction based on known risks and can be a useful guide for policy makers and public health officials.

They also found that the probability of a person experiencing a pandemic like COVID-19 in one's lifetime is around 38%. The researchers said this could double in years to come.

The probability of another pandemic is "going to probably increase because of all of the environmental changes that are occurring," Willian Pan, an associate professor of Global Environmental Health at Duke University and one of the study's authors, told ABC News.

Scientists are looking closely at the relationship between climate changes and zoonotic diseases, like COVID-19.

25. The key point of the passage is

(A) to encourage people to get vaccinated

(B) to inform people that a probability of another epidemic will be higher in the coming decades because of environmental changes

(C) to educate people to segregate their trash

(D) to invite people to move to another country with less likelihood of an epidemic

26. How much will the likelihood of an extreme epidemic increase in the coming decades according to the passage?

(A) twice   (B) multiple   (C) threefold   (D) quadruple

27. How was the likelihood of increased epidemic calculated?

(A) the researchers used the death rate of COVID-19

(B) the researchers use the response time of every country to the pandemic since 2020

(C) the researchers used the vaccination rate of each country

(D) the researchers used data from epidemics from the past 400 years, specifically death rates, length of previous epidemics, and the rate of new infectious diseases

28. To what does Willian Pan, an associate professor of Global Environmental Health at Duke University, associate the increased probability of another pandemic?

(A) the environmental changes that are occurring

(B) the resistance of the virus to treatments

(C) the population of the world

(D) the current medical advancements

29. What part of speech is the underlined word in line 2?

(A) adjective   (B) adverb   (C) verb   (D) preposition

30. What does the underlined word in line 10 mean?

(A) advanced   (B) late   (C) naïve   (D) crude

Questions 31–36

Over 300 years ago, Swiss physician Johannes Hofer observed disturbing behaviors among Swiss mercenaries fighting in far-flung lands. The soldiers were prone to anorexia, despondency and bouts of weeping. Many attempted suicide. Hofer determined that the mercenaries suffered from what he called "nostalgia," which he concluded was "a cerebral disease of essentially demonic cause."

Nowadays, nostalgia's reputation is much improved. Social psychologists define the emotion—which Hofer saw as synonymous with "homesickness"—as a sentimental longing for meaningful events from one's past. And research suggests that nostalgia can help people cope with dementia, grief and even the disorientation experienced by immigrants and refugees (SN: 3/1/21).

Nostalgia may even help people cope with the COVID-19 pandemic. In a study published September 8 in *Social, Psychological and Personality Science*, researchers found when some lonely, unhappy people reminisced about better, pre-pandemic moments, they felt happier. The results suggest that nostalgia can serve as an antidote to loneliness during the pandemic, the researchers conclude.

31. The key point of the passage is

    (A) to discourage people from feeling nostalgic

    (B) to educate people how nostalgia can help people cope with distress

    (C) to inform people that nostalgia is a mental illness

    (D) to advise people that nostalgia will cure their mental illness

32. According to the passage, what word is synonymous with nostalgia?

    (A) homesickness (B) loneliness (C) grief (D) misery

33. According to the study mentioned in the passage, how does nostalgia help people cope with the COVID-19 pandemic?

    (A) when people think of ways to spend their time with

    (B) when people feel homesick and decide to go back to their hometown

    (C) when people reminisce pre-pandemic moments, they feel happier

    (D) when people go for retail therapy

34. How was nostalgia defined 300 years ago?

    (A) sentimental longing for meaningful events from one's past

    (B) antidote to loneliness

    (C) cure to mental illness

    (D) a cerebral disease of essentially demonic cause by Swiss physician Johannes Hofer

35. What does the underlined word in line 23 mean?

    (A) remember with pleasure   (B) neglect   (C) intentionally forget   (D) omit from one's memory

36. What does the underlined word in line 26 mean?

    (A) poison   (B) toxin   (C) remedy   (D) sickness

End of section.

If you have any time left, go over the questions in this section only.

Do not start the next section.

You have 40 minutes to answer the 47 questions in the Mathematics Achievement Section.

Each question is followed by four suggested answers. Read each question and then decide which one of the four suggested answers is best.

Find the row of spaces on your document that has the same number as the question. In this row, mark the space having the same letter as the answer you have chosen. You may write in your test booklet.

SAMPLE QUESTION: Sample Answer

Which of the numbers below is not factor of 364?   A ● C D

(A) 13
(B) 20
(C) 26
(D) 91

The correct answer is 20, so circle B is darkened.

---

1. Which of the following is divided by 7?

(A) $45 \times 4 - (40 \div 4) + 11 (3 + 7)$

(B) $33 \times 3 - (15 \div 4) + 4 (2 + 9)$

(C) $59 \times 2 - (43 \div 4) + 11 (3 + 2)$

(D) $46 \times 1 - (51 \div 5) + 0 (1 + 7)$

2. What is the least common multiple of 7, 14, and 19?

(A) 363   (B) 588   (C) 931   (D) 1,021

3. $19 \times 25 = 254 + $ _____.

(A) 323   (B) 233   (C) 111   (D) 221

4. $\dfrac{3}{5} \times \dfrac{7}{15} =$

(A) $\dfrac{7}{25}$ (B) $\dfrac{5}{15}$ (C) $\dfrac{3}{20}$ (D) $\dfrac{7}{20}$

5. In triangle QRS, find the value of $x°$.

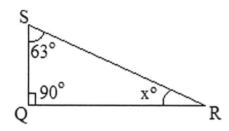

(A) 30° (B) 27° (C) 33° (D) 50°

6. $21^3 =$?

(A) 9,621 (B) 9,261 (C) 9,126 (D) none of the above

7. Find the value of tan 4° tan 43° tan 47° tan 86°

(A) 1 (B) $\dfrac{1}{2}$ (C) 2 (D) $\dfrac{2}{3}$

8. Ten percent discount and then 20% discount in succession is equivalent to total discount of:

(A) 15% (B) 30% (C) 24% (D) 28%

9. The perimeter of one face of a cube is 20 cm. Its volume will be:

(A) 100 cm³ (B) 125 cm³ (C) 400 cm³ (D) 625 cm³

10. What sum of money will become $1,352 in two years at 4% p.a. compound interest?

(A) $1,200 (B) $1,225 (C) $1,250 (D) $1,300

11. Allowing 20% and 15% successive discounts, the selling price of an article becomes $3,060, then the marked price will be:

(A) $4,400 (B) $5,000 (C) $4,500 (D) $4,000

12. Which of the following is equivalent to $\dfrac{25}{13}x = 12 + 2y$?

(A) $5x - 27y = 169$ (B) $15x - 13y = 163$ (C) $15x - 13y = 144$ (D) $25x - 26y = 156$

13. $30 \times 0.59 =$?

(A) 16.02 (B) 18.02 (C) 18.39 (D) 17.39

14. If $\sin^2\theta + \sin\theta = 1$, then find the value of $(\cos^4\theta + \cos^2\theta)$.

(A) 1 (B) 2 (C) 0 (D) $\sqrt{2}$

15. If $\dfrac{a}{b} + \dfrac{b}{a} = 2$, then what is the value of $(a + b)^2$?

(A) $2ab$ (B) $4ab$ (C) $8ab$ (D) 4

Questions 16–21

Refer to the following graph.

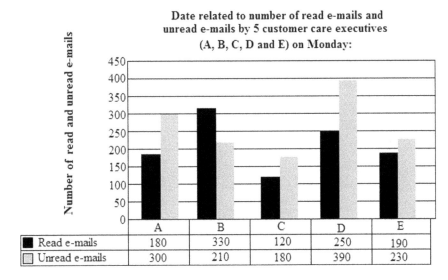

Date related to number of read e-mails and unread e-mails by 5 customer care executives (A, B, C, D and E) on Monday:

	A	B	C	D	E
Read e-mails	180	330	120	250	190
Unread e-mails	300	210	180	390	230

Note: (I) Number of received e-mails = Number of read e-mails + number of unread e-mails

(II) No pending e-mails from previous days to be considered for calculation. Data is related to the number of e-mails received on Monday only.

16. The number of e-mails read by B is what percent more than that read by D?

(A) 36 (B) 32 (C) 24 (D) 28

17. Out of the e-mails read by B, 60% are from male customers. The number of unread e-mails from female customers is 51 less than that of read e-mails from female customers, what is the number of unread e-mails from male customer?

(A) 127 (B) 131 (C) 133 (D) 129

18. The number of e-mails received by F was 38% more than that by C and number of e-mails read by F was 25% more than that unread by him, how many e-mails were read by F?

(A) 230 (B) 220 (C) 240 (D) 210

19. What is the difference between number of received e-mails by A and that by E?

(A) 50   (B) 60   (C) 70   (D) 80

20. Percentage of read e-mails out of received e-mails (each of them) were equal for A and G. If the number of e-mails received by G is 360, how many e-mails were unread by G?

(A) 225   (B) 215   (C) 220   (D) 230

21. What is the average number of received e-mails by D and E?

(A) 540   (B) 550   (C) 530   (D) 520

22. $510{,}151 - 119 \div 17 - x^2 = 80$

(A) 4   (B) 10   (C) 8   (D) 12

23. $36.24 \div 3$

(A) 13.02   (B) 13.80   (C) 12.05   (D) 12.08

24. Find the wrong number of the given series
462   422   380   342   306

(A) 422   (B) 380   (C) 342   (D) 306

25. Two trains leave NYC for WC at 6 p.m. and 6:30 p.m. Their speeds are 60 km/hr and 75 km/hr, respectively. At what distance (in km) from NYC will the two trains meet?

(A) 67.5   (B) 150   (C) 75   (D) 60

26. Find the missing number

3	4	5
2	3	5
1	2	3
14	29	?

(A) 50   (B) 30   (C) 40   (D) 32

27. $3 \times 16^{\frac{3}{4}} = ?$

(A) 20   (B) 22   (C) 24   (D) 25

28. If $\dfrac{x}{x+1} = \dfrac{4}{5}$, what is the value of x?

(A) 4   (B) 5   (C) 6   (D) 7

29. $\dfrac{9.5 \times 0.085}{0.0017 \times 0.19} = ?$

(A) 2,500 (B) 250 (C) 25 (D) 5

30. What number is the cube of 6 divided by 3?

(A) 84 (B) 72 (C) 96 (D) 108

31. The product of two numbers is 4,107. If the H.C.F. of the numbers is 37, the L.C.M is:

(A) 185 (B) 111 (C) 107 (D) 101

32. By selling a headphone for $950, I lose 5%. What percent shall I gain by selling it for $1,040?

(A) 5 (B) 4 (C) 4.5 (D) 9

33. Find the L.C.M. of 13, 39, and 52.

(A) 160 (B) 320 (C) 169 (D) 156

34. Find the H.C.M. of 51, 68, and 85.

(A) 13 (B) 5 (C) 18 (D) 17

35. $\dfrac{9,261 \times 20 \times 20 \times 20}{21 \times 21 \times 21} = ?$

(A) 6,240 (B) 6,000 (C) 8,000 (D) 9,000

36. 8 : 69 : : 7 : ?

(A) 55 (B) 56 (C) 57 (D) 54

37. Find the suitable alternative to complete the series?
1, 4, 9, 16, 25, _____?

(A) 49 (B) 35 (C) 36 (D) 48

38. The L.C.M. of two numbers is 864 and their H.C.F. is 144. If one of the numbers is 288, then the other number is:

(A) 432 (B) 576 (C) 144 (D) 1,296

39. The compound interest on a sum of money for two years is $615 and the simple interest for the same period is $600. Find the principle.

(A) 6,000 (B) 6,500 (C) 8,000 (D) 9,500

40. Twelve kilograms of rice costing 30 per kg is mixed with 8 kg of rice costing $40 per kg. The price of mixed rice is:

(A) 95   (B) 78   (C) 29   (D) 34

41. 16,000 + 18,594 – 3,556 = ?

(A) 56,245   (B) 50,000   (C) 31,038   (D) 30,000

42. $2^8 - 3^4 = ?$

(A) 100   (B) 125   (C) 145   (D) 175

43. Which of the following is correct for the value $\dfrac{12.225}{12.334}$

(A) $\dfrac{12,225 \times 100}{12,334 \times 100}$ (B) $\dfrac{122,250}{123,340}$ (C) $\dfrac{1,225}{1,234}$ (D) none of the above

44. $s^2 - 2st + t^2 = ?$

(A) $(s - t)^2$ (B) $(s + t)^2$ (C) $s^2 - t^2$ (D) $s^2 + t^2$

45. If $x = 2$ and $y = 6$, find the value of $2x + 3y^4$.

(A) 3,593   (B) 3,399   (C) 3,892   (D) 2,857

46. If $s = 30.06$ and $t = 12.6$, then find the value of st.

(A) 322.152   (B) 378.756   (C) 188.265   (D) 985.265

47. What is value of: 8 u 2 r 7 f 1 i 0, if u = +, r = ÷, f = –, i = ×

(A) 0.26   (B) 14   (C) 0   (D) 21

End of section.

If you have any time left, go over the questions in this section only.

Do not start the next section.

Essay Topic Sheet

The directions for the Essay portion of the ISEE are printed in the box below. Use the pre-lined pages on pages 37 and 38 for this part of the Practice Test.

You will have 30 minutes to plan and write an essay on the topic printed on the other side of this page. **Do not write on another topic. An essay on another topic is not acceptable.**

The essay is designed to give you an opportunity to show how well you can write. You should try to express your thoughts clearly. How well you write is much more important than how much you write, but you need to say enough for a reader to understand what you mean.

You will probably want to write more than a short paragraph. You should also be aware that a copy of your essay will be sent to each school that will be receiving your test results. You are to write only in the appropriate section of the answer sheet. Please write or print so that your writing may be read by someone who is not familiar with your handwriting.

You may make notes and plan your essay on the reverse side of the page. Allow enough time to copy the final form onto your answer sheet. You must copy the essay topic onto your answer sheet, in the box provided.

Please remember to write only the final draft of the essay on your answer sheet and to write it in blue or black pen. Again, you may use cursive writing or you may print. Only pages 37 and 38 will be sent to the schools.

Directions continue on the next page.

REMINDER: Please write this essay topic on the first few lines of your answer sheet.

Essay Topic

> If you were given a chance to reincarnated as an animal, what would you be and why?

- Only write on this essay question
- Only pages 37 and 38 will be sent to the schools
- Only write in blue or black pen

NOTES

STUDENT NAME _____ GRADE APPLYING FOR _____

Use a blue or black ballpoint pen to write the final draft of your essay on this sheet.

You must write your essay topic in this space.

_____

_____

_____

Use specific details in your response

_____

_____

_____

_____

_____

_____

_____

_____

_____

_____

_____

_____

_____

_____

_____

_____

_____

_____

_____

_____

End of section.

If you have any time left, go over the questions in this section only.

ANSWER KEY

Verbal Reasoning

1. A	9. C	17. B	25. A	33. D
2. A	10. B	18. A	26. B	34. B
3. B	11. D	19. C	27. C	35. C
4. B	12. C	20. D	28. D	36. D
5. C	13. A	21. A	29. B	37. A
6. D	14. B	22. B	30. B	38. C
7. D	15. C	23. C	31. C	39. A
8. A	16. D	24. D	32. A	40. D

1. The correct answer is (A). To adjudicate means to make a formal judgment or decision about a problem or disputed matter. Synonyms are to decide, resolve, and settle.

2. The correct answer is (A). Adroit means clever or skillful in using the hands or mind. Synonyms are skillful, adept, and dexterous.

3. The correct answer is (B). Analogous means comparable in certain respects, typically in a way which makes clearer the nature of the things compared. Synonyms are comparable, parallel, and similar.

4. The correct answer is (B). To assimilate means to take in (information, ideas, or culture) and understand fully. Synonyms are to incorporate, adopt, and embrace.

5. The correct answer is (C). To avert means to turn away one's eyes or thoughts or prevent or ward off (an undesirable occurrence). Synonyms are to prevent, stop, and avoid.

6. The correct answer is (D). To bemoan means to express discontent or sorrow over (something). Synonyms are lament, bewail, detest, and deplore.

7. The correct answer is (D). To be brazen is to be bold and without shame. Synonyms are forward, brash, and bold.

8. The correct answer is (A). To be brusque means to be abrupt or offhand in speech or manner. Synonyms are curt, blunt, and sharp.

9. The correct answer is (C). To be canny means having or showing shrewdness and good judgment, especially in money or business matters. Synonyms are clever, wise, and sensible.

10. The correct answer is (B). To capitulate means to cease to resist an opponent or an unwelcome demand, surrender. Synonyms are surrender, yield, and submit.

11. The correct answer is (D). Defunct means no longer existing or functioning. Synonyms are unused, obsolete, and extinct.

12. The correct answer is (C). Expanse means an area of something, typically land or sea, presenting a wide continuous surface. Synonyms are stretch, space, and extent. Sample: "the green expanse of the forest"

13. The correct answer is (A). Implicit means implied though not plainly expressed. Synonyms are indirect, suggested, and tacit.

14. The correct answer is (B). Inimical means tending to obstruct or harm. Synonyms are harmful, detrimental, and destructive.

15. The correct answer is (C). Notorious means famous or well known, typically for some bad quality or deed. Synonyms are infamous, scandalous, and prominent.

16. The correct answer is (D). To maul means to wound (a person or animal) by scratching and tearing or to treat (someone or something) roughly. Synonyms are attack, mutilate, and mangle.

17. The correct answer is (B). To mortify means to cause (someone) to feel embarrassed, ashamed, or humiliated. Synonyms are to embarrass, humiliate, and horrify.

18. The correct answer is (A). Peevish means easily irritated, especially by unimportant things. Synonyms are irritable, moody, and grumpy.

19. The correct answer is (C). To rebuke means to express sharp disapproval or criticism of (someone) because of their behavior or actions. Synonyms are scold, reprimand, and criticize.

20. The correct answer is (D). To reverberate means to (of a loud noise) be repeated several times as an echo. Synonyms are echo, resonate, and rumble.

21. The correct answer is (A). A boondoggle refers to a work or activity that is wasteful or pointless but gives the appearance of having value. In American Political slang, it means an extravagant and useless project. In this sentence, the man's mother did not approve of his hobbies which she considered as pointless activities.

22. The correct answer is (B). A caveat is a care taken to avoid danger or mistakes, a warning. In this sentence, the birds' actions felt like they were giving a warning to the speaker that something terrible is coming.

23. The correct answer is (C). Concomitant means naturally accompanying or associated. Synonyms are associated, related, and linked. Sample: "She loved travel, with all its concomitant worries." In this sentence, the subject took the opportunity despite the associated uncertainties of moving into a new city.

24. The correct answer is (D). To constrain means to compel or force (someone) to follow a particular course of action. In this sentence, children are compelled to care for their parents.

25. The correct answer is (A). To restrain means to prevent (someone or something) from doing something; keep under control or within limits. In this sentence, the staff were prevented from walking out of the restaurant.

26. The correct answer is (B). To engender means to cause or give rise to (a feeling, situation, or condition). In this sentence, it is about time that the actions cause a riot from the townspeople.

27. The correct answer is (C). To indict means to formally accuse of or charge with a serious crime. In this sentence, after the mayor was charged for corruption, the reputable vice mayor supervised new projects.

28. The correct answer is (D). Intransigent means unwilling or refusing to change one's views or to agree about something. In this sentence, Carla remained firm to pursue acting.

29. The correct answer is (B). Mayhem means violent or damaging disorder, chaos. In this sentence, the speaker shared how she can't imagine adding one more child because having three has already left her house in a complete disorder.

30. The correct answer is (B). To muster means to collect or assemble (a number or amount). In this sentence, the speaker is saying that one needs to collect a lot of courage if one wishes to pursue this path.

31. The correct answer is (C). Pecuniary means relating to or consisting of money. In this sentence, her grandfather arranged her marriage to a rich man because of financial interests.

32. The correct answer is (A). Plight means a dangerous, difficult, or otherwise unfortunate situation. In this sentence, the speaker is urging the audience to put effort in saving our children from the trouble or mess, of our generation's actions.

33. The correct answer is (D). To plummet means to decrease rapidly in value or amount. In this sentence, the subject's reputation crashed when the town knew that she disliked charity.

34. The correct answer is (B). To quench means to satisfy (one's thirst) by drinking. In this sentence, the subject went for days without water to drink.

35. The correct answer is (C). Zenith means the time at which something is most powerful or successful. In this sentence, just as when the subject was the top of her career, a scandal ruined her reputation.

36. The correct answer is (D). Mirth means amusement, especially as expressed in laughter. In this sentence, the subject jumped in amusement upon seeing his favorite childhood movie.

37. The correct answer is (A). To pelt means to attack (someone) by repeatedly hurling things at them. In this sentence, two little boys attacked/repeatedly threw rotten tomatoes at the man.

38. The correct answer is (C). To perturb means to make (someone) anxious or unsettled. In this sentence, Damien's arrogance upset the ladies at court.

39. The correct answer is (A). To retort means to repay (an insult or injury). In this sentence, Anna finally had the courage to respond to Lucy's bullying.

40. The correct answer is (D). To wince is to give a slight involuntary grimace or shrinking movement of the body out of or in anticipation of pain or distress. In this sentence, the singer who was anxious flinched at the sight of the crowd.

Quantitative Reasoning

1. C	11. D	21. C	31. B
2. A	12. C	22. D	32. D
3. B	13. D	23. A	33. B
4. B	14. B	24. A	34. C
5. B	15. A	25. B	35. A
6. D	16. A	26. B	36. A
7. C	17. C	27. A	37. A
8. C	18. A	28. B	
9. C	19. B	29. B	
10. C	20. B	30. D	

1. The correct answer is (C). Multiplication of 68 and 9 is 612.

2. The correct answer is (A). Half of the perimeter = {(20 × 4) ÷ 2} = 40 ft.

3. The correct answer is (B). 6 × 7 × 14 − (7 × 7 × 6 × 2) = 588 − 588 = 0.

4. The correct answer is (B). Average = {(88 + 85 + 95 + 60 + 74) ÷ 5} = 80.40.

5. The correct answer is (B).

    The pattern is:

    $7 \times 1 + 1 = 7 + 1 = 8$

    $8 \times 2 + 2 = 16 + 2 = 18$

    $18 \times 3 + 3 = 54 + 3 = 57$

    $57 \times 4 + 4 = 228 + 4 = 232$

    $232 \times 5 + 5 = 1,160 + 5 = 1,165$

6. The correct answer is (D). $\dfrac{63}{9} \div \dfrac{27}{81} = \dfrac{63}{9} \times \dfrac{81}{27} = 7 \times \dfrac{9}{3} = 7 \times 3 = 21.$

7. The correct answer is (C). $\dfrac{5x}{5} + 13 = \dfrac{5.9}{5} + 13 = \dfrac{45}{5} + 13 = 9 + 13 = 22.$

8. The correct answer is (C). $\sqrt[4]{256} = \sqrt[4]{4 \times 4 \times 4 \times 4} = 4.$

9. The correct answer is (C).

    $151.04 - 118.95 \div 17.01 - x^2 = 80.07$

    ® $151.04 - 6.99 - x^2 = 80.07$

    ® $144.05 - x^2 = 80.07$

    ® $144.05 - x^2 = 80.07 - 144.05$

    ® $x^2 = 63.98$

    ® $x = 7.9987....$ (Ans.)

10. The correct answer is (C)

    $\dfrac{3}{8} = \dfrac{3 \times 15}{8 \times 15} = \dfrac{45}{120} = 45$

    $\dfrac{1}{4} = \dfrac{1 \times 30}{4 \times 30} = \dfrac{30}{120} = 30$

    $\dfrac{5}{6} = \dfrac{5 \times 20}{6 \times 20} = \dfrac{100}{120} = 100$

    $\dfrac{3}{10} = \dfrac{3 \times 6}{10 \times 6} = \dfrac{18}{120} = 18$

    As, 100 is greater than all of the above values, so $\dfrac{5}{6}$ is the answer.

11. The correct answer is (D). The number of events held in Hall C → 210 – 35 = 175.

    The number of events held in Hall D → 280 – 55 = 225.

    ∴ Required ratio = 175:225 = 7:9.

12. The correct answer is (C).

    The number of events held in Hall E → 265 – 25 = 240.

    ∴ Non-marriage reception events → $\dfrac{240 \times 15}{100} = 36$

    The number of events held in Hall A → 242 – 32 = 210.

    ∴ Non-marriage reception events → $\dfrac{210 \times 20}{100} = 42$

    ∴ Required percent = $\left(\dfrac{42 - 36}{42}\right) \times 100 = \dfrac{6}{42} \times 100 = \dfrac{100}{7} = 14\dfrac{2}{7}\%$

13. The correct answer is (D).

    The number of events held in Hall B in 2016 → 254 – 30 = 224.

    ∴ Number of events held in 2018 → $\dfrac{30 \times 120}{100} = 36$.

    ∴ Number of events booked = 252 + 36 = 288.

14. The correct answer is (B).

    Number of marriage receptions held:

    Hall A → $\dfrac{210 \times 80}{100} = 168$

    Hall B → $\dfrac{224 \times 75}{100} = 168$

    Hall D → $\dfrac{225 \times 80}{100} = 180$

    ∴ Required average

    $= \dfrac{168 + 168 + 180}{3} = \dfrac{516}{3}$

    $= 172$

15. The correct answer is (A). Required difference = (210 + 240) – (32 + 35) = 450 – 57 = 393.

16. The correct answer is (A). The pattern in this series is made by adding consecutive odd numbers 3,5,7,9 ... from each number to get next number so 63 + 9 =72.

17. The correct answer is (C). $44 \div 0.11 = 400$.

18. The correct answer is (A).

    $3x + 1 = 7$

    ® $x = 6 \div 3$

    ® $x = 2$.

    $420x + x = 20 \times 2 + 2 = 42$.

19. The correct answer is (B). $78 \times 78 = 6{,}084$.

20. The correct answer is (B). $9{,}24{,}580 = 9{,}00{,}000 + 20{,}000 + 4{,}000 + 500 + 80 + 0$.
    So, the answer is 80.

21. The correct answer is (C). Here $x = 180° – 140° = 40°$, therefore two quantities are equal.

22. The correct answer is (D). The relationship cannot be determined from this information because we cannot find x and y individually with this information, we only have $xy = 18$.

23. The correct answer is (A). Here $\sqrt{16} + \sqrt{49} = 11$ and $\sqrt{16 + 49} = 8.062$, therefore Column A is greater.

24. The correct answer is (A). Here the area is 18, one side of the quadrilateral is 3, then the other side will be 6. Now the perimeter will be $= 2 \times (6 + 3) = 18$ unit. So, Column A is greater.

25. The correct answer is (B). Martha had \$4. She gave half of her money to her sister so now she has $= \$2$. Also, Linda has now \$3. So, Column B is greater.

26. The correct answer is (B). Here $4x + 11 = 67$, then $4x = 56$, so $x = 14$, and $\frac{y}{3} = 12$, then $y = 36$.

27. The correct answer is (A). The area of the rectangle $= 7 \times 4 = 28$ sq. unit and the area of the square $= 5 \times 5$ sq. unit $= 25$ sq. unit. Therefore, Column A is greater.

28. The correct answer is (B). The average number of cookies $= 2$, and the number of cookies eaten on Thursday is 3. So, Column B is greater.

29. The correct answer is (B). Here 8.1 > 0.81, therefore $\sqrt{8.1} > \sqrt{0.81}$.

30. The correct answer is (D). The relationship cannot be determined from the information which is given in this question. Here we don't know the price for one orange and one peach.

31. The correct answer is (B). Here $-(7)^6 = -1,17,649$ and $(-7)^6 = 1,17,649$, hence Column B is greater.

32. The correct answer is (D). The relationship cannot be determined from the information given. Because there are 11, 13 those are odd and A can be any one of them and there are 10, 12, 14 that are even and B can be any one of them, so it is undetermined.

33. The correct answer is (B). The prime numbers are 1, 3, 5, 7, 11 and the odd numbers are 1, 3, 5, 7, 9, 11. So the probability of odd number is greater than the probability of prime numbers.

34. The correct answer is (C). The fractional part of the figure that is shaded $= \dfrac{3}{20}$, hence two quantities are equal.

35. The correct answer is (A). 50% of 16 slices = 0.5 × 16 = 8 and one-fourth of the pizza = 0.25 × 16 = 4. Therefore, Column A is greater.

36. The correct answer is (A). 80% of $40 = $32 and 80% of $32 = $25.6 and 60% of $40 = $24, hence Column B is greater.

37. The correct answer is (A). The slope $= \dfrac{8-2}{5-4} = 6$ and $3x - y = -8$, then $y = 3x + 8$, therefore the slope = 3. So, Column A is greater.

Reading Comprehension and Vocabulary

1.	A	7.	A	13.	B	19.	D	25.	B	31.	B
2.	A	8.	A	14.	B	20.	C	26.	C	32.	A
3.	D	9.	D	15.	D	21.	B	27.	D	33.	C
4.	C	10.	B	16.	A	22.	A	28.	A	34.	D
5.	B	11.	C	17.	B	23.	A	29.	B	35.	A
6.	D	12.	A	18.	C	24.	C	30.	A	36.	C

1. The correct answer is (A). The passage is about how strong the U.S. dollar is currently. As explained in lines 20–24, the U.S. dollar can buy more Japanese yen currently. $1 dollar can buy 143 Japanese yen which is about 30% more than a year ago.

2. The correct answer is (A). See lines 1–4, 20–24.

3. The correct answer is (D). See lines 20–24. Consider the Japanese yen. A year ago, $1 could get a little less than 110 yen. Now, it can buy 143.

4. The correct answer is (C). See lines 29–31. The U.S. Dollar index, which measures the dollar against the euro, yen, and other major currencies, has climbed more than 14% this year.

5. The correct answer is (B). See lines 5–10. Not all six currencies are listed and known in this passage.

6. The correct answer is (D). If something eases off, or a person or thing eases it off, it is reduced in degree, speed, or intensity.

7. The correct answer is (A). The passage aims to educate people where the particular kind of poliovirus was detected, the link of the vaccination rate to the places infected by the virus, and how the virus spread.

8. The correct answer is (A). Vietnam is not mentioned in the passage. See lines 6–8.

9. The correct answer is (D). Somerset is not mentioned in the passage. According to the passage, the virus is detected in New York and Somerset is a county in New Jersey.

10. The correct answer is (B). See lines 15–18. This spurred wastewater surveillance in Rockland and the surrounding counties because people shed poliovirus in their stool.

11. The correct answer is (C). See lines 29–31. While most people infected with polio don't have symptoms, some might feel like they have the flu, with fever, fatigue, or a sore throat.

12. The correct answer is (A). See lines 31–35. In rare cases, the virus can cause permanent paralysis, and the disease can turn deadly if that paralysis hits the muscles that control breathing or swallowing.

13. The correct answer is (B). The passage discusses the mangrove restoration effort of Kenya and the environmental benefits you get from mangroves which include preventing soil erosion; protection against tropical storms; serving as habitats to birds, fish, and other animals; and absorbing carbon.

14. The correct answer is (B). See lines 1–6. Mikoko Pamoja, launched in 2013, is the world's first mangrove-driven carbon credit initiative. It earned the United Nations' Equator Prize in 2017, awarded for innovative solutions to poverty that involve conservation and sustainable use of biodiversity.

15. The correct answer is (D). All the choices are the benefits you get from mangrove as discussed in the passage. The passage discusses the mangrove restoration effort of Kenya and the environmental benefits you get from mangroves which include preventing soil erosion; protection against tropical storms; serving as habitats to birds, fish, and other animals; and absorbing carbon.

16. The correct answer is (A). See lines 27–28. Speckling these roots are thousands of specialized pores or lenticels.

17. The correct is (B). See lines 18–19. The trees can grow up to 27 m tall.

18. The correct answer is (C). To thrive means to prosper, flourish. Sample: "education groups thrive on organization"

19. The correct answer is (D). The passage describes a phenomenon which the writer of the passage calls a blursday. According to a theory written by a psychologist and his team, we lose definition of time when our temporal landmarks disappear because time is typically punctuated by events, such as dinner dates or daily commutes.

20. The correct answer is (C). See lines 10–15. Welcome to "blursday." Back when the pandemic started, the term hit the zeitgeist. The word captured that sense of time disintegrating as our worlds and routines turned upside down (SN: 9/14/20). Days melted together, then weeks, then years.

21. The correct answer is (B). Out of whack means out of order; not working. Sample: "all their calculations were out of whack"

22. The correct answer is (A). See lines 17–20. Simon Grondin, a psychologist at Laval University in Quebec City, and colleagues penned a theory paper seeking to explain the phenomenon.

23. The correct answer is (A). See lines 20–26. Our time is typically punctuated by events, such as dinner dates or daily commutes, Grondin and his team wrote in October 2020 in *Frontiers in Psychology*. Such events provide temporal landmarks. When those landmarks disappear, days lose their identities. Time loses its definition.

24. The correct answer is (C). See line 23.

25. The correct answer is (B). The passage talks about how the probability of epidemic will increase in the coming years according to research. Researchers have associated this likelihood to climate change. Scientists are studying the relationship between climate changes and zoonotic diseases, like COVID-19. See lines 23–25.

26. The correct answer is (C). See lines 1–5. The likelihood of an extreme epidemic, or one similar to COVID-19, will increase threefold in the coming decades, according to a recent study published in the *Proceedings of the National Academy of Sciences*.

27. The correct answer is (D). See lines 6–9. The researchers used data from epidemics from the past 400 years, specifically death rates, length of previous epidemics, and the rate of new infectious diseases.

28. The correct answer is (A). See lines 17–22. The probability of another pandemic is "going to probably increase because of all of the environmental changes that are occurring," Willian Pan, an associate professor of Global Environmental Health at Duke University and one of the study's authors, told ABC News.

29. The correct answer is (B). Threefold can be used as an adjective or an adverb. It means by three times: three times the number or amount. In this line, the word threefold is an adverb modifying the verb "increase."

30. The correct answer is (A). Sophisticated means (of a machine, system, or technique) developed to a high degree of complexity.

31. The correct answer is (B). The passage talks about how nostalgia can help people cope with the COVID-19 pandemic, and other mental illnesses such as dementia, grief, and disorientation experienced by immigrants. The results of the research suggest that that nostalgia can serve as an antidote to loneliness during the pandemic.

32. The correct answer is (A). See lines 12–13.

33. The correct answer is (C). See lines 22–24.

34. The correct answer is (D). See lines 8–9.

35. The correct answer is (A). To reminisce means to indulge in enjoyable recollection of past events.

36. The correct answer is (C). An antidote is a medicine taken or given to counteract a particular poison. It also means something that counteracts or neutralizes an unpleasant feeling or situation.

Mathematics Achievement

1. A	11. C	21. C	31. B	41. C
2. C	12. D	22. C	32. B	42. D
3. D	13. D	23. D	33. D	43. A
4. A	14. A	24. A	34. D	44. A
5. B	15. B	25. B	35. C	45. C
6. B	16. B	26. A	36. D	46. B
7. A	17. D	27. C	37. C	47. B
8. D	18. A	28. A	38. A	
9. B	19. B	29. A	39. A	
10. C	20. A	30. B	40. D	

1. The correct answer is (A).

   $45 \times 4 - (40 \div 4) + 11 (3 + 7) = 180 - 10 + 11 \times 10 = 180 - 10 + 110 = 280$.

   280 is divisible by 7.

2. The correct answer is (C).

   931 is divisible by 7, 14, and 19.

3. The correct answer is (D).

   $19 \times 25 = 475$

   $475 - 254 = 221$

4. The correct answer is (A).

   $$\frac{3}{5} \times \frac{7}{15} = \frac{7}{25}$$

5. The correct answer is (B).

   We know the total value of all angles of a triangle is 180°.

   So, $180° - (90° + 63°) = 27°$.

6. The correct answer is (B).

   $21^3 = 21 \times 21 \times 21 = 9,261$.

7. The correct answer is (A).

   tan 4° . tan 43° tan 47° . tan 86°

   = tan (90° − 86°) × tan (90° − 47°) × tan 47° × tan 86°

   = tan 86° × cot 47° × tan 47° × tan 86° = 1.

8. The correct answer is (D).

   As per rules $\left[x + y + \dfrac{xy}{100} \right]\%$

   $= -10 - 20 + \dfrac{(-10 \times -20)}{100} = -30 + 2 = 28\%$

9. The correct answer is (B).

   Perimeter of one face, $4a$ = 20 cm

   Side of a cube = a = 5 cm

   Volume of cube = a^3 = $(5)^3$ = 125 cm^3

10. The correct answer is (C).

    Let the sum = x

    $4.1352 = x\left(1 + \dfrac{4}{100}\right)^2$

    or, $1,352 = x\left(\dfrac{26}{25}\right)^2$

    or, $x = \dfrac{1,352 \times 25,125}{26 \times 26}$

    or, $x = \$1,250$.

11. The correct answer is (C).

    S.P. of an article = 20% and 15%

    Successive discount × Marked price of an article

    or, $3,060 = \dfrac{80}{100} \times \dfrac{85}{100} \times$ Marked Price

    Marked price of an article = $\dfrac{3,060 \times 100 \times 100}{80 \times 85} = \$4,500$.

12. The correct answer is (D).

$$\frac{25}{13}x = 12 + 2y$$

® $25x = 156 + 26y$

® $25x - 26y = 156.$

13. The correct answer is (D). $30 \times 0.59 = 17.7.$

14. The correct answer is (A).

$\sin^2\theta + \sin\theta = 1$

® $\sin\theta = 1 - \sin^2\theta = \cos^2\theta$

$\cos^4\theta + \cos^2\theta = (\cos^2\theta)^2 + \cos^2\theta = \sin^2\theta + \cos^2\theta = 1.$

15. The correct answer is (B).

$a^2 + b^2 = 2ab$ ® $(a - b)^2 = 0$

$(a - b)^2 = (a + b)^2 + 4ab = 4ab.$

16. The correct answer is (B).

Required percent

$$= \frac{330 - 250}{250} \times 100 = \frac{800}{25} = 32\%.$$

17. The correct answer is (D).

E-mails received by B from males $= \dfrac{330 \times 60}{250} = 198$

E-mails from female customers $= 330 - 198 = 132$

Unread e-mails $= 210$

Unread e-mails received from females $= 132 - 51 = 81$

4 Unread e-mails received from males $= 210 - 81 = 129.$

18. The correct answer is (A).

E-mails received by F $= \dfrac{300 \times 138}{100} = 414$

Unread e-mails $= x$

4 Read e-mails $= \dfrac{5x}{4}$

$$4x + \frac{5x}{4} = 414$$

$$® \frac{9x}{4} = 414 ® x = \frac{414 \times 4}{9} = 184$$

4 Read e-mails $= \frac{5 \times 184}{9} = 230$

19. The correct answer is (B).

Required difference = (300 + 180) – (190 + 230) = 480 – 420 = 60

20. The correct answer is (A).

Percentage of e-mails read by A $= \frac{180}{480} \times 100 = 37.5$

4 E-mails unread by G $= (100 - 37.5)\%$ of $360 = \frac{360 \times 625}{100} = 225$

21. The correct answer is (C).

Required Average $= \frac{250 + 390 + 190 + 230}{2} = \frac{1,060}{2} = 530$

22. The correct answer is (C).

$151 - 119 \div 17 - x^2 = 80$

$®151 - 7 - x^2 = 80$

$® x^2 = 144 - 80 = 64$

$x = \sqrt{64} = 8$

23. The correct answer is (D). $36.24 \div 3 = 12.08$.

24. The correct answer is (A).

462 – 42 = 420

420 – 40 = 380

380 – 38 = 342

342 – 36 = 306

So, the number 422 is wrong in this series.

25.   The correct answer is (B).

Let, after covering x km both train meet

So, $\dfrac{x}{60} = \dfrac{x}{75} + \dfrac{1}{2}$

or, $\dfrac{x}{60} = \dfrac{2x + 75}{150}$

or, $\dfrac{x}{2} = \dfrac{2x + 75}{150}$

$4\ 5x = 4x + 150$

$4\ x = 150$

So, distance is 150 km.

26.   The correct answer is (A).

$(3)^2 + (2)^2 + (1)^2 = 14$

So, $(5)^2 + (4)^2 + (3)^2 = 25 + 16 + 9 = 50$

27.   The correct answer is (C).

$3 \times (16)^{\frac{3}{4}} = 3 \times \left(2^4\right)^{\frac{3}{4}} = 3 \times 2^3 = 24$

28.   The correct answer is (A).

$\dfrac{x}{x+1} = \dfrac{4}{5}$ ® $5x = 4x + 4$ ® $x = 4$

29.   The correct answer is (A).

$\dfrac{9.5 \times 0.085}{0.0017 \times 0.19} = \dfrac{95 \times 85 \times 100}{17 \times 19} = 2,500.$

30.   The correct answer is (B).

The cube of 6 is 216. 216 divided by 3 = 72.

31.   The correct answer is (B).

L.C.M. $= \dfrac{4,107}{37} = 111$

Hence the L.C.M. = 111.

32. The correct answer is (B).

CP of the tape recorder $= \dfrac{100}{95} \times 950 = \$1,000$

Gain $= \$1,040 - \$1,000 = \$40$

4 Gain percent $= \dfrac{40}{100} \times 100 = 4\%$

33. The correct answer is (D). L.C.M. of 13, 39, and 52 is 156.

34. The correct answer is (D). H.C.M. of 51, 68, and 85 is 17.

35. The correct answer is (C). $\dfrac{9,261 \times 20 \times 20 \times 20}{21 \times 21 \times 21} = 8,000$

36. The correct answer is (D).

$8 \times 8 = 64, \; 64 + 5 = 69$

Similarly, $7 \times 7 = 49, \; 49 + 5 = 54$.

37. The correct answer is (C). $1 + 3 = 4; \; 4 + 5 = 9; \; 9 + 7 = 16; \; 16 + 9 = 25; \; 25 + 11 = \underline{36}$.

38. The correct answer is A.

First Number × Second Number = H.C.F. × L.C.M.

$288 \times S = 864 \times 144$

$S = 432$

39. The correct answer is (A).

Simple interest for one year = 300

Interest on $300 = (615 - 600) = \$15$

Rate $= \dfrac{15 \times 100}{300 \times 1} = 5\%$

Simple interest $= \dfrac{P \times 5 \times 2}{100} = 600$

® P = $6,000.

40. The correct answer is (D).

$(12 \times 30 + 8 \times 40) = 680$

Average per kg price $= \dfrac{680}{20} = 34$.

41.   The correct answer is (C).

    16,000 + 18,594 – 3,556 = 34,594 – 3,556 = 31,038

42.   The correct answer is (D).

    $2^8 - 3^4 = 256 - 81 = 175$.

43.   The correct answer is (A).

    $$\frac{12.225}{12.334} = \frac{12,225 \times 100}{12,334 \times 100}$$

44.   The correct answer is (A).

    As, $(a + b)^2 = a^2 + 2ab + b^2$,

    So, $(s + t)^2 = s^2 + 2st + t^2$

45.   The correct answer is (C).

    $x = 2$ and $y = 6$

    So, $2x + 3y^4 = (2 \times 2) + (3 \times 6^4) = 4 + (3 \times 1,296) = 4 + 3,888 = 3,892$.

46.   The correct answer is (B).

    $s = 30.06$ and $t = 12.6$

    So, $st = 30.06 \times 12.6 = 378.756$.

47.   The correct answer is (B).

    $u = +, r = \div, f = -, i = \times$

    $8\ u\ 2\ r\ 7\ f\ 1\ i\ 0 = 8 + 42 \div 7 - 1 \times 0 = 14$.

Sample Essay Response

Many cultures believed that there is something beyond death. Reincarnation is one of them. It is a belief that the soul or the non-physical essence of a living being begins a new life in another physical form after death. This belief also sees that the soul or non-physical being is immortal and the body is only a perishable vessel.

I have mixed feelings about reincarnation whether I will believe it or not, but if I will be reincarnated as an animal, I would choose to be a bird. I think a lot of people would either choose to be a dog or a cat since they are the most common house pets. Some people may choose to be a lion because lions are called kings of the jungle. To be a bird is the least of the answers I expect from people when they are asked the same question because most birds are seen locked up in a cage and are tiny little beings. A bird may not have a long life as the other animals, but it is its freedom that I want to experience.

If I get reincarnated as a bird, I will be able to flap my wings and fly. My wings can take me to places I've never been. I will be the first to see a storm coming in the sky. I will be the first to feel the rain as I fly through the clouds. Nature will provide what I need, and I will never have to worry about food, shelter, or clothing. I will never have to worry about keeping up with the inflation, hospital costs and expectations from others. I will never have to meet anyone's standards.

People's answer will, if not all, be related to their current life experience or situation. Someone may choose to be a panda because they long for the attention that pandas get. Someone may choose to be a sloth because they envy the slow lives sloths have. Like every generational household, at least where I am from, I've been raised to be a good child. To be a good child means to finish college with flying colors, get a stable job and give back to your parents for raising you. Being an eldest child also means you must set as a good example to your younger siblings. It is expected that your parents will be tougher on you. Following a different path means that you are a bad child therefore, exploring your individuality is far-fetched. You can only either be like your parents, be someone that your parents didn't become, a doctor, or a lawyer. In families like mine, being unconventional is not allowed. This may be the reason why some children decide to cut off ties. Some will stay and continue what they call the norm in their future families. To be an animal in general is to be carefree of the world's prejudice. However, to be a bird is to be a symbol of freedom and that's what I desire the most. To be free from all these expectations is what I want if I ever have a second life.

As the saying goes, free as a bird.

For the ISEE, the most commonly referenced score is the stanine score. Check out the four steps to calculating stanine scores.

Step 1: The Raw Score

The first step in scoring is calculating a raw score. This is quite simple.

Students receive one point for each correct answer and no points for incorrect answers or unanswered questions.

Tip: Because there is no score penalty for incorrect answers or unanswered questions, be sure to answer every single question! Answering all of the questions can only increase your chances of a higher score.

Step 2: The Scaled Score

Once a raw score has been calculated for each section, it is converted into a scaled score.

This conversion adjusts for the variation in difficulty between different tests. Thus, a lower raw score on a harder test could give you the same scaled score as a higher raw score on an easier test. This process is called equating.

The scaled score for each section ranges from 760 to 940.

Step 3: The Percentile Score

Next, the percentile score for each section is calculated.

Percentiles compare a student's scaled score to all other same-grade students from the past three years. This is important to understand because the ISEE is taken by students in a range of grades. The Upper Level ISEE, for instance, is taken by students applying to grades 9–12; however, the percentile score is based only on the performance of other students applying to the same grade. Thus, a student applying to 9th grade will not be compared to a student applying to 12th grade.

1st   50th   99th

Here's an example to help understand percentile scores: scoring in the 40th percentile indicates that a student scored the same or higher than 40% of students in the same grade but lower than 59% of students.

Step 4: The Stanine Score

Finally, the percentile is converted into a stanine score.

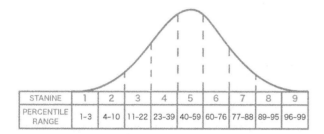

STANINE	1	2	3	4	5	6	7	8	9
PERCENTILE RANGE	1–3	4–10	11–22	23–39	40–59	60–76	77–88	89–95	96–99

Notice that the percentile ranges for the middle stanines of 4–6 are far larger than the ranges for the extreme stanines of 1, 2, 8, or 9. This means that most students taking the ISEE achieve scores in the middle ranges. Only the top 4% of all test takers receive a stanine of 9 on any given section, while 20% of students receive a stanine of 5.

So, what is a good ISEE score?

Stanine scores (which range from 1 to 9) are the most important and are the scores schools pay the most attention to. But what is a good score on the ISEE? A score of 5 or higher will be enough to put students in the running for most schools, although some elite private schools want applicants to have ISEE test results of 7 or higher.

Here's a sample ISEE Report

Individual Student Report

Candidate for Grade	**8**
ID Number	
Gender	**Male**
Date of Birth	**4/8/2004**
Phone Number	
Test Level/Form	**Middle/0916**
Date of Testing	**11/30/2016**
Tracking Number	**201612010592103**

The Test Profile below shows your total scores for each test. Refer to the enclosed brochure called *Understanding the Individual Student Report* to help you interpret the *Test Profile* and *Analysis*. Percentile Ranks and Stanines are derived from norms for applicants to independent schools.

TEST PROFILE

Section	Scaled Score (760 – 940)	Percentile Rank (1 – 99)	Stanine (1 – 9)	Stanine Analysis 1 2 3 4 5 6 7 8 9
Verbal Reasoning	895	90	8	V
Reading Comprehension	890	76	6	R
Quantitative Reasoning	894	81	7	Q
Mathematics Achievement	883	61	6	M

LEGEND: V = Verbal Reasoning   R = Reading Comprehension   Q = Quantitative Reasoning   M = Mathematics Achievement

ANALYSIS

Section & Subsection	# of Questions	# Correct	Results for Each Question
Verbal Reasoning			
Synonyms	18	15	+++++++++- ++++- ++- +
Single Word Response	17	16	+++++++++++- +++++
Quantitative Reasoning			
Word Problems	18	11	+++- - - +++- +++++- - -
Quantitative Comparisons	14	14	++++++++++++++
Reading Comprehension			
Main Idea	4	4	++++
Supporting Ideas	6	5	- +++++
Inference	6	5	+- ++++
Vocabulary	7	5	+++- +- +
Organization/Logic	4	4	++++
Tone/Style/Figurative Language	3	3	+++
Mathematics Achievement			
Whole Numbers	7	4	+- +++- -
Decimals, Percents, Fractions	9	5	++- - ++- - +
Algebraic Concepts	11	7	+++++- ++- - -
Geometry	4	2	+- +-
Measurement	5	4	++++-
Data Analysis and Probability	6	4	+++- +-

LEGEND: + = Correct   - = Incorrect   S = Skipped   N = Not Reached

The test was administered in the order reported in the analysis section; Verbal Reasoning, Quantitative Reasoning, Reading Comprehension, and Mathematics Achievement. Each section was divided into subsections, grouping similar types of questions. The Reading Comprehension subsection grouping does not represent the actual order of the test questions.

The above is a preliminary ISEE report. ERB reserves the right to amend this report before it is finalized. The report will be final no later than 20 business days. The final report will automatically be generated electronically.

ISEE—Middle Level Exam-2

Verbal Reasoning

You have 20 minutes to answer the 40 questions in the Verbal Reasoning Section.

This section is divided into two parts that contain two different types of questions. As soon as you have completed Part I, answer the questions in Part II. You may write in your test booklet. For each answer you select, fill in the corresponding circle on your answer document.

Part I—Synonyms

Each question in Part I consists of a word in capital letters followed by four answer choices. Select the one word that is most nearly the same in meaning as the word in capital letters.

SAMPLE QUESTION: Sample Answer

CHARGE: A   B   ●   D

(A) release
(B) belittle
(C) accuse
(D) conspire

Part II—Sentence Completion

Each question in Part II is made up of a sentence with one blank. Each blank indicates that a word or phrase is missing. The sentence is followed by four answer choices. Select the word or phrase that will best complete the meaning of the sentence as a whole.

SAMPLE QUESTIONS: Sample Answer

It rained so much that the streets were _____.   ●   B   C   D

(A) flooded
(B) arid
(C) paved
(D) crowded

The house was so dirty that it took _____.   A   B   C   ●

(A) less than 10 min to wash it
(B) four months to demolish it
(C) over a week to walk across it
(D) two days to clean it

Part I—Synonyms

Directions:

Select the word that is most nearly the same in meaning as the word in capital letters.

1. ELIGIBLE

   (A) desirable (B) immature (C) raw (D) amateur

2. OBSCURE

   (A) clear (B) illegible (C) readable (D) vivid

3. DROUGHT

   (A) abundance (B) wealth (C) lack (D) adequacy

4. REBUFF

   (A) welcome (B) embrace (C) accept (D) refuse

5. SHACKLE

   (A) restrain (B) indulge (C) avoid (D) accept

6. STANCE

   (A) handwriting (B) stand (C) reflection (D) fashion

7. STINT

   (A) generously (B) adequate (C) restrict (D) allow

8. DERISION

   (A) recognition (B) acknowledgment (C) praise (D) insult

9. PRATTLE

   (A) pause (B) prove (C) silence (D) chatter

10. WHET

(A) spoil (B) dull (C) sharpen (D) dispose

11. TEMPEST

(A) calm (B) tranquility (C) chaos (D) peace

12. SOLILOQUY

(A) announcement (B) monologue (C) discourse (D) chat

13. MIDDLING

(A) huge (B) average (C) exceptional (D) outstanding

14. MEDDLING

(A) interfering (B) ignoring (C) letting (D) allowing

15. NARY

(A) not (B) alert (C) different (D) block

16. ABSTRUSE

(A) obvious (B) crystal (C) cryptic (D) apparent

17. ATHWART

(A) front (B) back (C) across (D) below

18. SPURIOUS

(A) mad (B) genuine (C) real (D) counterfeit

19. REPINE

(A) purify (B) mourn (C) cleanse (D) filter

20. ADULATION

(A) devotion (B) hatred (C) indifference (D) disloyalty

Part II—Sentence Completion

Directions:

Select the word that best completes the sentence.

21. She has always loved the peace of silence, so she hated the _____ type.

    (A) garrulous   (B) reserved   (C) modest   (D) quiet

22. The police strive to put the _____ behind bars.

    (A) miscreant   (B) innocent   (C) youth   (D) victim

23. Since he was a child, he has always wanted to be a _____ man.

    (A) ordinary   (B) puissant   (C) average   (D) poor

24. There were piles of _____ left after the music festival and they were almost of juice boxes, water bottles, and food packaging.

    (A) display   (B) artifact   (C) exhibit   (D) riffraff

25. Andrea started to _____, looking hurt by what her friend had said to her.

    (A) laugh   (B) snivel   (C) smile   (D) jump

26. In a small box, he kept a _____ gift that nobody noticed but it was special to Kaye.

    (A) big   (B) trifling   (C) lavish   (D) fancy

27. Nobody befriended him because he always had a _____ look until he cut his hair short and started wearing brighter colors.

    (A) bright   (B) clean   (C) dingy   (D) striking

28. The teacher realized, to her _____ that nobody has done their assignments over the break.

    (A) chagrin   (B) delight   (C) passive   (D) intransigent

29. The emperor's plan turned into a _____ after a spy spilled the details to the enemy.

    (A) fiasco   (B) success   (C) hit   (D) smash

30. His brother's lifelong goal is to _____ them with books borrowed from his master so that they become successful in life.

    (A) bore (B) edify (C) mislead (D) punish

31. The waves were strong and the boat violently _____ which made him lose his footing.

    (A) steadied (B) anchored (C) lurched (D) docked

32. The king prepared a party for the entire kingdom to attend to _____ its heroes of the war.

    (A) banish (B) despise (C) mock (D) exalt

33. Behind her fan, she _____ at the gentleman's words of admiration.

    (A) simpered (B) cackled (C) bawled (D) roared

34. According to urban legends, the house is haunted by a tall, _____ woman in black.

    (A) plump (B) gaunt (C) chubby (D) stout

35. Never trust the _____ waters of a small lake for you never know what's lurking beneath.

    (A) stormy (B) rough (C) placid (D) shallow

36. He took her hand, and her cheeks became _____ from embarrassment.

    (A) dingy (B) purple (C) pale (D) ruddy

37. Because he was too shy to say hello to his new classmates, he spent his free time _____ about the school corridors.

    (A) skulking (B) shouting (C) avoiding (D) painting

38. Due to lack of experience, she _____ her first attempt to bake a wedding cake for her first client.

    (A) bungled (B) succeed (C) passed (D) aced

39. He is unable to _____ paying his due bills after they've piled up for months of delinquency.

    (A) detest (B) evade (C) endanger (D) escalate

40. Their pregnancy announcement has the family's _____ congratulations.

    (A) hostile (B) frosty (C) hearty (D) frigid

End of section.

If you have any time left, go over the questions in this section only.

Do not start the next section.

You have 35 minutes to answer the 37 questions in the Quantitative Reasoning Section.

Each question is followed by four suggested answers. Read each question and then decide which one of the four suggested answers is best.

Find the row of spaces on your document that has the same number as the question. In this row, mark the space having the same letter as the answer you have chosen. You may write in your test booklet.

EXAMPLE 1:   <u>Sample Answer</u>

What is the value of the expression (4 + 6) ÷ 2?   A   B   ●   D

(A) 2
(B) 4
(C) 5
(D) 7

The correct answer is 5, so circle C is darkened.

EXAMPLE 2:

A square has an area of 25 cm². What is the length of one of its   A   ●   C   D
side?

(A) 1 cm
(B) 5 cm
(C) 10 cm
(D) 25 cm

The correct answer is 5 cm, so circle B is darkened.

---

1. If "+" means "minus," "–" means "multiply," "÷" means "plus," and "×" means "divide," then $10 \times 5 \div 3 - 2 + 3 = ?$

   (A) 5   (B) $\dfrac{53}{5}$ (C) 21   (D) 36

2. What is the smallest value among these?

   $\dfrac{3}{8}, \dfrac{1}{4}, \dfrac{5}{6}, \dfrac{3}{10}$

   (A) $\dfrac{3}{8}$ (B) $\dfrac{1}{4}$ (C) $\dfrac{5}{6}$ (D) $\dfrac{3}{10}$

3. What is the value of the digit 9 in the number 9,24,580?

   (A) 0.90,000   (B) 9,00,000   (C) 9,00.000   (D) 9.00.000

4. $6^2 + 8^2 =$

   (A) 13^2 (B) 12^2 (C) 11^2 (D) 10^2

5. Examine the best answer.

   (P) 6^3

   (Q) 3^6

   (R) $2^3 \times 6^3$

   (A) (P) × (Q) is greater than (R)   (B) (P) – (Q) is an irrational number

   (C) (P) is the greatest number   (D) none of these.

6. Find circumference of the circle whose diameter is 5 cm.

   (A) 10π cm   (B) 5π cm   (C) 25π cm   (D) 50π cm

7. $97 \times 57 =$

   (A) 9,216   (B) 5,529   (C) 6,012   (D) 5,782

Questions 8–12

Study the following information carefully and answer the questions given below.

A word and number arrangement machine when given an input line of words and numbers rearranged them following a particular rule in each step. The following is an illustration of input and rearrangement.

Input: cup for hot 34 69 72 tea 27

Step I: 27 cup for hot 34 69 72 tea

Step II: 27 tea cup for hot 34 69 72

Step III: 27 tea 34 cup for hot 69 72

Step IV: 27 tea 34 hot cup for 69 72

Step V: 27 tea 34 hot 69 cup for 72

Step VI: 27 tea 34 hot 69 for cup 72

Step VII: 27 tea 34 hot 69 for 72 cup

And Step VII is the last step of the above arrangement.

As per the rules followed in the above steps, find out in each of the following question the appropriate step for given input.

8. Input: Kind 12 96 heart water 59 42 yes

   How many steps will be required to complete the rearrangement?

   (A) three   (B) five   (C) four   (D) six

9. Input: jungle 43 mode 25 basket 39 target 19

   Which of the following steps will be the last but one?

   (A) VII   (B) VIII   (C) IX   (D) none of the above

10. Step III of an input is: 12 world 31 ask cart ball 87 75

    Which of the following will definitely be the input?

    (A) 31 ask cart ball 87 75 world 12   (B) 31 ask cart ball 87 75 12 world

    (C) 31 ask 12 world cart ball 87 75   (D) Cannot be determined

11. Step II of an input is: 24 year 56 43 last part 64 over

    How many more steps will be required to complete the rearrangement?

    (A) four   (B) six   (C) seven   (D) five

12. Step III of an input: 32 station 46 81 73 march go for is:

    (A) 32 station 46 march 73 go for 81   (B) 32 station 46 march 73 81 go for

    (C) 32 station 46 march 73 go 81 for 4.   (D) none of the above

13. Find the correct one.

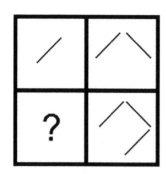

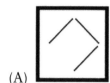 (A)   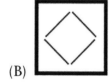 (B)   (C)   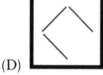 (D)

14. Consider the following Venn diagram.

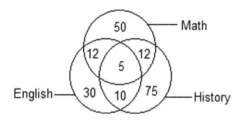

Five hundred candidates appeared in an examination comprising of tests in English, Mathematics, and History. The diagram gives the number of the candidates who failed in different tests. What is the percentage of the candidates who failed in at least two subjects?

(A) 0.078   (B) 1.0   (C) 6.8   (D) 7.8

15. $(7 \times 6 \div 2) - 6 \times 7 \div 14 =$

(A) 100   (B) 18   (C) −15   (D) 8

16. If $4x + 2 = 22$, then what is the value of $20x + 18$?

(A) 118   (B) 150   (C) 132   (D) 140

17. If $x = 9$, then find the value of $\dfrac{x^2}{5} + 13$

(A) 13   (B) 9   (C) 18   (D) 26

18. What is the half of the perimeter of a square with a side of 60 ft?

(A) 124 ft   (B) 150 sq. ft   (C) 130 ft   (D) 180 ft

19. $\sqrt[8]{256} = ?$

(A) 128   (B) 85   (C) 4   (D) 2

20. $\dfrac{63}{7} \div \dfrac{21}{35} =$

(A) 6.40   (B) 5   (C) 2.08   (D) 5.40

Part II—Quantitative Comparisons

Directions:

Using all information given in each question, compare the quantity in Column A to the quantity in Column B. All questions in Part II have these answers choice:

(A)   the quantity in Column A is greater

(B)   the quantity in Column B is greater

(C)   the two quantities are equal

(D)   the relationship cannot be determined from the information given

21.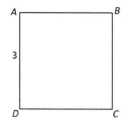

Column A	Column B
x	120

22. A rectangle with sides x and y has an area of 24.

Column A	Column B
The length of x	The length of y

23.

Column A	Column B
$\sqrt{25} + \sqrt{49}$	$\sqrt{49 + 25}$

24.

The quadrilateral $ABCD$ has an area of 9.

Column A	Column B
The perimeter of $ABCD$	15

25. John had \$10. He gave half of her money to her sister, Jenny. Jenny now has \$15.

Column A	Column B
The amount of money John now has	The amount of money Jenny had originally

26. $2x + 5 = 63$

$\dfrac{y}{2} + 6 = 15$

Column A	Column B
x	y

27.

Column A	Column B
The area of a rectangle with length 3 and width 4	The area of a a square with a side of 5

28. Number of Chocolates Eaten Each Day

Wednesday	3
Thursday	1
Friday	2
Saturday	2

Column A	Column B
The average number of chocolates eaten each day	The number of chocolates eaten on Friday

29.

Column A	Column B
$\sqrt{0.49}$	$\sqrt{4.9}$

30. Amy bought nine oranges and seven peaches.

The total price of the fruit was \$1.60.

Column A	Column B
The cost of one orange	The cost of one peach

31.

Column A	Column B
$-(8)^6$	$(-8)^6$

32. *a* represents an odd integer greater than 9 and less than 15.
b represents an even integer greater than 9 and less than 15.

Column A	Column B
$a \times 3$	$b \times 4$

33. A 12-sided die with faces numbered 1–12 is rolled.

Column A	Column B
The probability that the result is even	The probability that the result is prime

34.

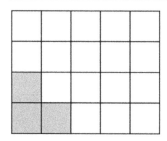

Column A	Column B
The fractional part of the figure that is shaded	$\dfrac{3}{20}$

35. Melvin brought a large pizza with 16 slices.

Column A	Column B
The number of slices left if Melvin eats 50% of the pizza	The number of slices left if Melvin eats one-fourth of the pizza

36. The original price of a phone case that is now on sale was $40.

Column A	Column B
The price of the case after two 20% discount	The price of the case after a single 40% Discount

37.	Column A	Column B
	The slope of the line with points (4,2) and (5, 8)	The slope of the line $3x - y = -8$

End of section.

If you have any time left, go over the questions in this section only.

Do not start the next section.

You have 25 minutes to answer the 36 questions in the Reading Comprehension and Vocabulary section.

Directions:

This section contains six short reading passages. Each passage is followed by six questions based on its content. Answer the questions following each passage on the basis of what is stated or implied in that passage. You may write in your test booklet.

Questions 1–6

Some seabirds don't just survive storms. They ride them.

Streaked shearwaters nesting on islands off Japan sometimes head straight toward passing typhoons, where they fly near the eye of the storm for hours at a time, researchers report in the Oct. 11 *Proceedings of the National Academy of Sciences*. This strange behavior—not reported in any other bird species—might help streaked shearwaters (*Calonectris leucomelas*) survive strong storms.

Birds and other animals living in areas with hurricanes and typhoons have adopted strategies to weather these deadly storms (SN: 10/2/15). In recent years, a few studies using GPS trackers have revealed that some ocean-dwelling birds—such as the frigatebird (*Fregata minor*)—will take massive detours to avoid cyclones.

This is an understandable strategy for birds that spend most of their time at sea where "there is literally nowhere to hide," says Emily Shepard, a behavior ecologist at Swansea University in Wales. To find out whether shearwaters also avoid storms, she and her colleagues used 11 years of tracking data from GPS locators attached to the wings of 75 birds nesting on Awashima Island in Japan.

By combining this information with data on wind speeds during typhoons, the researchers discovered that shearwaters that were caught out in the open ocean when a storm blew in would ride tailwinds around the edges of the storm. However, others that found themselves sandwiched between land and the eye of a strong cyclone would sometimes veer off their usual flight patterns and head toward the center of the storm.

1. The main objective of this passage is

(A) to inform readers how a species of birds can survive a strong storm by heading toward the center of the storm

(B) to persuade the readers to buy this bird as they have adopted a survival strategy against storms

(C) to advertise streaked shearwaters in the market

(D) to invite more people to study the behavior of birds

2. What species of bird is the focus of the passage?

(A) seabirds (B) mallard (C) Swansea (D) bald eagle

3. Which country are the shearwaters the researchers studied from?

(A) Fregata (B) Japan (C) Wales (D) Awashima Island

4. What behavior makes this species of bird different from the others?

(A) they would ride tailwinds around the edges of the storm

(B) they are caught out in the open ocean

(C) they would ride the storm

(D) they would find a safe place to hide in a sea cave or by the beach

5. According to a behavior ecologist, how does this species of bird develop this coping strategy to survive strong storms?

(A) it's their usual flight patterns

(B) because of climate change

(C) by spending most of their time at sea where there is nowhere to hide

(D) because they are being tracked using GPS locators

6. What does the underlined phrasal verb mean in line 36?

(A) stay in course (B) go back to where you came from

(C) stare into the space (D) go in the wrong/different direction

Questions 7–12

Ninna Ragasa was 24 years old when doctors discovered a mass on the left hemisphere of her brain. Further imaging revealed that Ragasa had an arteriovenous malformation, a tangle of blood vessels that disrupt the flow of oxygen to the brain.

Doctors suggested removing the mass to avoid the possibility of it rupturing, a potentially fatal outcome. Ragasa, a graduate student in interior design at the Pratt Institute in New York City, worried that the brain surgery would hurt her mobility and her career aspirations.

"Being a designer came easily to me," says Ragasa, who is a friend of mine.

But the procedure went smoothly, and Ragasa returned to her life at Pratt. Then a year or so after the surgery, Ragasa started falling. At first, she blamed her hard-work, hard-party lifestyle and cut back on drinks. But she kept falling. So, she switched from spike heels to chunky boots and then to flip flops. Nothing helped. One day Ragasa fell getting off the subway and had to crawl to her mother's house.

Scans revealed that Ragasa's brain had swelled after the procedure, causing her to gradually lose mobility along the right side of her body. Ragasa could no longer handle the physical demands of being an art student, such as building models and drawing. So, she dropped out of school and found a job that came with medical insurance to pay for her physical therapy treatments. She felt, she says, totally lost.

Many of us get derailed at some point in our lives. We may get sick like Ragasa, divorced, laid off or lose a loved one. Our age when calamity strikes can profoundly influence our response to the event, research suggests, with young adults particularly vulnerable to getting thrown off course. That's partially because when the rites of passage that mark the transition from childhood to adulthood are delayed or lost, young adults can feel unmoored and increasingly uncertain about the future—a point driven home by this cohort's plummeting well-being during the ongoing pandemic.

7. The key point of the passage is

   (A) to introduce a designer who had a brain mass

   (B) to share that our age can influence our response when calamity strikes by sharing Ninna's story

   (C) to convince people not to get a surgery   (D) to prove that younger generations are mentally weak

8. How is Ninna Ragasa significant to the passage?

   (A) Ninna's story was used in the passage as a sample of how young adults are vulnerable to be thrown off course when faced by a calamity

   (B) Ninna is a famous icon who is used as an inspirational character in the passage

   (C) Ninna is the headlines of the news   (D) Ninna is nobody

9. What medical condition did Ragasa have?

   (A) brain mass   (B) frequent falling   (C) loss of mobility   (D) hypertension

10. How did Ragasa lose her mobility?

    (A) a virus attacked her brain after surgery   (B) a bacteria attacked her brain after surgery

    (C) her brain swelled after the procedure   (D) she kept falling off

11. According to the passage, what is the relationship of one's age influence in response to a calamity when it strikes?

    (A) Nothing. Age is just a number

    (B) it can influence our response to events in our life such as when a calamity strikes

    (C) this generation's young adults are not emotionally strong compared to prior generations

    (D) the younger you are, the less mature your decisions are

12. In line 43, what does the underlined word mean?

    (A) coward   (B) anxious   (C) positive   (D) confused

Questions 13–18

The small motorboat anchors in the middle of the Chesapeake Bay. Shrieks of wintering birds assault the vessel's five crew members, all clad in bright orange flotation suits. One of the crew slowly pulls a rope out of the water to retrieve a plastic tube, about the length of a person's arm and filled with mud from the bottom of the bay.

As the tube is hauled on board, the stench of rotten eggs fills the air.

"Chesapeake Bay mud is stinky," says Sairah Malkin, a biogeochemist at the University of Maryland Center for Environmental Science in Cambridge who is aboard the boat. The smell comes from sulfuric chemicals called sulfides within the mud. They're quite toxic, Malkin explains.

Malkin and her team venture out onto the bay every couple of months to sample the foul muck and track the abundance of squiggling mud dwellers called cable bacteria. The microbes are living wires: Their threadlike bodies—thinner than a human hair—can channel electricity.

Cable bacteria use that power to chemically rewire their surroundings. While some microbes in the area produce sulfides, the cable bacteria remove those chemicals and help prevent them from moving up into the water column. By managing sulfides, cable bacteria may protect fish, crustaceans, and other aquatic organisms from a "toxic nightmare," says Filip Meysman, a biogeochemist at the University of Antwerp in Belgium. "They're kind of like guardian angels in these coastal ecosystems."

13. The key point of the passage is

   (A) to encourage people to visit Chesapeake Bay

   (B) to educate people how a certain bacterium from Chesapeake Bay mud is helping the ecosystem

   (C) to discourage people from going to Chesapeake Bay because of the stinky mud

   (D) to persuade people to buy a motorboat

14. According to the passage, what makes Chesapeake Bay mud stinky?

   (A) human waste   (B) dead sea creatures   (C) sulfides   (D) oil spill

15. What significant work did Malkin and her team do every couple of months in Chesapeake Bay?

   (A) track the abundance of cable bacteria which may protect sea creatures from toxic chemicals

   (B) prevent extinction of a species of fish

   (C) promote tourism at Chesapeake Bay   (D) none of the above

16. What is the importance of cable bacteria found in the Chesapeake Bay mud to the ecosystem?

    (A) they make the mud stinky

    (B) they prevent predators from attacking the aquatic life in the area

    (C) they can be a source of electricity   (D) they protect aquatic organisms from toxic sulfides

17. In line 3, what does the underlined word mean?

    (A) shining   (B) dressed   (C) seated   (D) held

18. In line 8, what does the underlined word mean?

    (A) unload   (B) pull   (C) put a hole   (D) make whole

Questions 19–24

Thousands of years ago, wolves bred with black dogs. The tryst didn't just give some of today's wolves a black coat—it has also helped them survive in parts of North America where a measles like virus can run rampant, according to a new study. That's because gray wolves are more likely to mate with black wolves when this virus is present—a rare demonstration in the wild of how pathogens can drive evolution.

"This paper takes a very elegant approach to understanding a fundamental question in biology: how animals choose mates," says Rena Schweizer, an evolutionary biologist at the University of Montana, Missoula, who was not involved with the work.

Humans aren't the only animals that show off their bodies to lure mates. Brighter bills in blackbirds and zebra finches do the same thing. One key signal in these species is color: The pigment that gives them their brilliant hues also improves their immune system, flagging to mates they're a good catch.

But researchers scoffed at the idea that black coloring could do the same thing, says Alexandre Roulin, an evolutionary biologist at the University of Lausanne.

Meanwhile, scientists had long puzzled over why there are more black wolves in Mexico than in Canada, or why they're more numerous farther south and in the Rocky Mountains. Tim Coulson and Sarah Cubaynes wondered whether their genes had something to do with it.

In 2011, Coulson, an evolutionary biologist at the University of Oxford, showed black wolves carrying just one copy of the gene variant that gives them their coat color survived better than black wolves with two copies of the variant and gray wolves with none. What's more, other work had shown the variant involved, known as CBD103, played a role in the immune systems of dogs.

19. The key point of the passage is

(A) to educate people how black coat in wolves is not just fashionable but played a role in survival

(B) to warn people of the existence of more dangerous wolves

(C) to advertise crossbreeding of wolves and black dogs

(D) to prove that black is more enticing

20. According to the passage, when did wolves bred with black dogs?

(A) during the pandemic   (B) in the Ice Age

(C) thousands of years ago   (D) since the beginning of time

21. What is the significance of wolves' black coat?

(A) flagging mates and helped them survive a virus

(B) they look fashionable

(C) they become more targeted in the fashion industry for their coat

(D) nothing significant with having black coat compared to standard gray

22. In line 2, what does the underlined word mean?

(A) fight   (B) agreement   (C) encounter   (D) mating

23. In line 11, what part of speech is the underlined word?

(A) noun   (B) pronoun   (C) verb   (D) adjective

24. In line 23, what does the underlined phrasal verb mean?

(A) agreeable with   (B) mocked   (C) appreciated   (D) recognized

Questions 25–30

Tuna are Olympic-caliber fish. They can swim hundreds to thousands of kilometers, some even cross the Pacific Ocean and back. That would seem to make it difficult—if not impossible—to establish a marine reserve large enough to protect them. But a new study shows two kinds of tuna have become much more abundant in a large marine reserve near Hawaii, suggesting they and other long-distance swimmers can be sheltered from overfishing.

The new study "shows that we can protect fish and we can eat more of them too," says Darcy Bradley, a conservation scientist at the University of California, Santa Barbara, who was not involved. "That hasn't been shown in this way before—this is the first demonstration at a large scale."

Marine protected areas safeguard coral reefs and other sensitive habitat or species. Governments establish them after consulting with conservationists, marine industries, and local people. When funding is available, boats patrol smaller areas and planes, or satellites can keep an eye on large reserves. In addition to conserving biodiversity, marine parks can also be used as nurseries for commercial stocks of fish. The idea is that when fishing is prohibited, the population inside will grow faster and "spill over" into waters beyond the borders of the reserve.

25. The key point of the passage is

(A) to stop overfishing

(B) to encourage people to buy more tuna than other kinds of fish

(C) to educate people how marine reserves helped with increasing fish population

(D) to invite people to go to Hawaii

26. Which country was the basis of the new study?

(A) Hawaii   (B) The USA   (C) Pacific   (D) California

27. How can a marine reserve help increase fish population for consumption?

(A) fishermen will only fish the types that are more abundant and do not need conservation

(B) there will be less fisherman in the ocean due to more marine reserves

(C) the population of the fish will grow faster in the marine reserves and will spill over beyond the borders which will make them available for fishing

(D) there will be more tuna in marine reserves than any other fish

28. According to the passage, what did the new study show?

(A) the new study "shows that we can protect fish and we can eat more of them too"

(B) marine protected areas safeguard coral reefs and other sensitive habitat or other species population

(C) governments are now consulting conversationists, marine industries, and local people

(D) more marine reserves need funding

29. In line 24, what part of speech is the underlined word?

(A) adjective   (B) adverb   (C) noun   (D) preposition

30. In line 27, what does the underlined word mean?

(A) allowed   (B) forbidden   (C) open   (D) loose

Questions 31–36

In the new study, the researchers collected samples of breath and sweat from non-smokers who had not recently eaten or drank. Samples were collected both before and after a fast-paced arithmetic task, along with self-reported stress levels and objective physiological measures: heart rate (HR) and blood pressure (BP). Samples from 36 participants who reported an increase in stress because of the task and experienced an increase in HR and BP during the task, were shown to trained dogs within three hours of being collected. Four dogs of different breeds and breed-mixes had been trained, using a clicker as well as kibble, to match odors in a discrimination task. At testing, dogs were asked to find the participant's stress sample (taken at the end of the task) while the same person's relaxed sample (taken only minutes before, prior to the task starting) was also in the sample line-up.

Overall, dogs could detect and perform their alert behavior on the sample taken during stress in 675 out of 720 trials, or 93.75% of the time, much greater than expected by chance ($p < 0.001$). The first time they were exposed to a participant's stressed and relaxed samples, the dogs correctly alerted to the stress sample 94.44% of the time. Individual dogs ranged in performance from 90% to 96.88% accuracy.

The authors conclude that dogs can detect an odor associated with the change in Volatile Organic Compounds produced by humans in response to stress, a finding that tells us more about the human-dog relationship and could have applications to the training of anxiety and PTSD service dogs that are currently trained to respond predominantly to visual cues.

31. The key point of the passage is

(A) to encourage people to get dogs as pets and support animals

(B) to educate people that dogs can detect stress through smells

(C) to inform people the dangers of having dogs as pets

(D) to convince people to stop smoking

32. According to the passage, how was the research concluded?

(A) dogs are great house pets   (B) dogs do not like smokers

(C) dogs have strong sense of smell   (D) dogs can detect stress through odor

33. Who were the target participants of the research?

(A) non-smokers who had not recently eaten or drank

(B) middle-aged men and women of the working class

(C) children below seven years old

(D) people who have been experiencing PTSD

34. When were the samples used in the research taken?

(A) both before and after a fast-paced arithmetic task, along with self-reported stress levels and objective physiological measures: heart rate (HR) and blood pressure (BP)

(B) early in the morning

(C) just before lunch break

(D) at nighttime

35. What is the significance of the study regarding dogs being able to smell stress?

(A) that service dogs are ineffective to smokers

(B) that dogs have a strong sense of smell

(C) nothing significant than what science already knows

(D) the findings in the study can tell us more about the human–dog relationship and could have applications to the training of anxiety and PTSD service dogs that are currently trained to respond predominantly to visual cues

36. In line 31, what does the underlined word mean?

(A) solid   (B) evaporative   (C) standard   (D) intangible

End of section.

If you have any time left, go over the questions in this section only.

Do not start the next section.

Mathematics Achievement

You have 40 minutes to answer the 47 questions in the Mathematics Achievement Section.

Each question is followed by four suggested answers. Read each question and then decide which one of the four suggested answers is best.

Find the row of spaces on your document that has the same number as the question. In this row, mark the space having the same letter as the answer you have chosen. You may write in your test booklet.

SAMPLE QUESTION: Sample Answer

Which of the numbers below is not factor of 364?   A ● C D

(A) 13
(B) 20
(C) 26
(D) 91

The correct answer is 20, so circle B is darkened.

---

1. By selling of 20 books, a bookseller gained the selling price of four books as profit. His gain percent is:

   (A) 20%   (B) 25%   (C) 12%   (D) 30%

2. Eighteen kilograms of wheat costing 45 per kg is mixed with 7 kg of wheat costing $48 per kg. The price of mixed wheat is:

   (A) 19.05   (B) 78.66   (C) 84.23   (D) 45.84

3. What is the value of 9 r 2 s 10 t 7 u 21, when r = +, s = ÷, t = –, u = ×

   (A) –0.80   (B) –155.48   (C) –137.80   (D) –186.77

4. 1,510.04 – 118 ÷ 81 + 64 = ?

   (A) 412.40   (B) 10,014.22   (C) 1,572.58   (D) 1,285.52

5. 118 ÷ 11.5 = ?

   (A) 20   (B) 22.11   (C) 10.26   (D) 30.25

6. Find the suitable alternative to complete the series?

−5, −3, 1, 3. _____ ?

(A) 0 (B) 2 (C) 5 (D) 8

7. The G.C.M. of two numbers is 12 and their sum is 120. The number of such pairs of numbers is:

(A) 1 (B) 2 (C) 3 (D) 4

8. 15,000 + 21,588 ÷ ? = 20,397

(A) −2 (B) 0 (C) 2 (D) 4

9. The arrangement of the number $\sqrt{8}, \frac{17}{6}$ and $\frac{82}{29}$ in increasing order from left to right is:

(A) $\frac{82}{29}, \sqrt{8}, \frac{17}{6}$ (B) $\frac{17}{6}, \sqrt{8}, \frac{82}{29}$ (C) $\sqrt{8}, \frac{17}{6}, \frac{82}{29}$ (D) $\frac{82}{29}, \frac{17}{6}, \sqrt{8}$

10. Simplified value of $\dfrac{(0.98)^3 - (0.1)^3}{(0.98)^2 + (0.098) + (0.1)^2}$

(A) 0.88 (B) 0.90 (C) 0.10 (D) 1.19

11. In triangle QRS, find the value of $x°$.

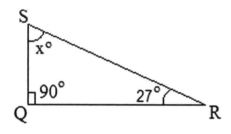

(A) 60° (B) 63° (C) 27° (D) 50°

12. $n^3 + 3n^2o + 3no^2 + o^3 = ?$

(A) $(n - o)^2$ (B) $(n + o)^2$ (C) $n^2 - o^2$ (D) $n^2 + o^2$

13. $3^8 - 3^5 = ?$

(A) 8,100 (B) 7,125 (C) 6,804 (D) 3,618

14. Find the missing number

(A) 7   (B) 42   (C) 9   (D) 1

Questions 15–20

Refer to the following graph.

Study the table carefully and answer the given questions.

Data regarding number of events booked/held at five different halls in 2016.

Halls	Number of Events Booked	Number of Events Cancelled	Out of Events Held, Percentage of Marriage Receptions
A	242	32	80%
B	254	30	75%
C	210	35	80%
D	280	55	80%
E	265	25	85%
Note: Number of events held = Number of events booked – Number of events cancelled.			

15. What was the respective ratio between number of events held at Hall C and those held at Hall D?

(A) 3:5   (B) 5:7   (C) 3:4   (D) 7:9

16. The number of events that were not marriage receptions at Hall E was what percent less than the number of events that were not marriage receptions at Hall A?

(A) $57\frac{1}{7}$ (B) $48\frac{1}{7}$ (C) $14\frac{2}{7}$ (D) $66\frac{2}{3}$

17. At Hall B in 2018, if number of events held was $1\frac{1}{8}$ times that in 2016 and number of events cancelled increased by 20% over that in 2016, how many events were booked?

(A) 282   (B) 278   (C) 284   (D) 288

18. What was the average number of marriage receptions held at Halls A, B, and D?

    (A) 158   (B) 156   (C) 148   (D) 172

19. What was the difference between total number of events held at Halls A and E together and those cancelled at the same halls together?

    (A) 393   (B) 383   (C) 403   (D) 398

20. A starts a certain business with $4,000. Three months from the start of the business, B joins with an amount which is $500 more than that invested by A. Nine months from the start of the business, B leaves and C joins, with an amount which is $1,500 more than that invested by B. If B's share from the annual profit is $18,000, what is the annual profit earned?

    (A) $64,000   (B) $72,000   (C) $62,000   (D) $54,000

21. In a school 40% of the students play football and 50% students play cricket. If 18% of the students neither play football nor cricket, then what is the percentage of the students playing both?

    (A) 40%   (B) 8%   (C) 2%   (D) 22%

22. Find the H.C.F. of 51, 68, and 85.

    (A) 13   (B) 5   (C) 18   (D) 17

23. $\dfrac{352 \times 21 \times 20 \times 21}{21 \times 21 \times 20} = ?$

    (A) 624   (B) 7,392   (C) 352   (D) 7,074

24. $209.44 \div 4$

    (A) 52.36   (B) 36.20   (C) 58   (D) 12.15

25. $19^3 = ?$

    (A) 6,201.11   (B) 6,859   (C) 915   (D) none of the above

26. $45 \div 0.59 = ?$

    (A) 16.02   (B) 97.02   (C) 81.39   (D) 76.27

27. Find the L.C.M. of 34, 68, and 102.

    (A) 160   (B) 220   (C) 269   (D) 204

28. If $x = 18$ and $y = 9$, find the value of $2x^2 + 3y$.

    (A) 959   (B) 399   (C) 677   (D) 287

29. $875 \div 25 = 254 - $ _____.

(A) 329 (B) 239 (C) 311 (D) 219

30. $\dfrac{2}{5}\% = ?$

(A) $\dfrac{1}{40}$ (B) $\dfrac{1}{125}$ (C) $\dfrac{1}{250}$ (D) $\dfrac{1}{500}$

31. Two trains leave Delhi for Kolkata at 6 p.m. and 6:30 p.m. Their speeds are 60 km/hr and 75 km/hr, respectively. At what distance (in km) from Delhi will the two trains meet?

(A) 67.5 (B) 150 (C) 75 (D) 60

32. If $\dfrac{x}{x+1} = \dfrac{4}{5}$, what is the value of x?

(A) 4 (B) 5 (C) 6 (D) 7

33. $9 : 81 :: 8 : ?$

(A) 50 (B) 63 (C) 60 (D) 64

34. If $s = 631.25$ and $t = 31.17$, then find the value of s/t.

(A) 22.15 (B) 20.25 (C) 18.25 (D) 35.65

35. $\dfrac{9.5 \times 0.85}{0.0017 \times 0.19} = ?$

(A) 902.5 (B) 250.6 (C) 555.5 (D) 500

36. Find the wrong number of the given series

462   420   370   336   294

(A) 370 (B) 336 (C) 294 (D) none of the above

37. The product of two numbers is 1,863. If the H.C.F. of the numbers is 27, the other number is:

(A) 50 (B) 69 (C) 111 (D) 121

38. If $\sin^2\theta + \sin\theta = 1$, then find the value of $(\cos^4\theta + \cos^2\theta)$.

(A) 1 (B) 2 (C) 0 (D) $\sqrt{2}$

39. What sum of money will become $1,352 in two years at 4% p.a. compound interest?

(A) $1,200 (B) $1,225 (C) $1,250 (D) $1,300

40. Ten percent discount and then 20% discount in succession is equivalent to total discount of:

(A) 15%   (B) 30%   (C) 24%   (D) 28%

41. What is the least common multiple of 6, 12, and 17?

(A) 1,063   (B) 1,088   (C) 1,224   (D) 1,226

42. $\dfrac{5}{6} \times \dfrac{36}{45} =$

(A) $\dfrac{2}{3}$ (B) $\dfrac{5}{15}$ (C) $\dfrac{3}{20}$ (D) $\dfrac{7}{20}$

43. The perimeter of one face of a cube is 32 cm. Its volume will be:

(A) 252 cm³   (B) 512 cm³   (C) 400 cm³   (D) 625 cm³

44. Which of the following is equivalent to $\dfrac{5}{13}x = 12 + 2y$?

(A) $5x - 27y = 169$ (B) $15x - 13y = 163$ (C) $15x - 13y = 144$ (D) $25x - 26y = 156$

45. If $\dfrac{a}{b} + \dfrac{b}{a} = 2$, then what is the value of $(a + b)^2$?

(A) $2ab$ (B) $4ab$ (C) $8ab$ (D) 4

46. Allowing 20% and 15% successive discounts, the selling price of an article becomes $3,060, then the marked price will be:

(A) $4,400   (B) $5,000   (C) $4,500   (D) $4,000

47. Which of the following is divided by 14?

(A) $45 \times 4 - (40 \div 4) + 11 (3 + 7)$ (B) $45 \times 3 - (15 \div 4) + 4 (2 + 7)$

(C) $59 \times 2 - (44 \times 4) + 14 (3 + 2)$ (D) $46 \times 11 \div (51 + 5) + 25 (1 \times 7)$

End of section.

If you have any time left, go over the questions in this section only.

Do not start the next section.

Essay Topic Sheet

The directions for the Essay portion of the ISEE are printed in the box below. Use the pre-lined pages on pages 103 and 104 for this part of the Practice Test.

You will have 30 minutes to plan and write an essay on the topic printed on the other side of this page. **Do not write on another topic. An essay on another topic is not acceptable.**

The essay is designed to give you an opportunity to show how well you can write. You should try to express your thoughts clearly. How well you write is much more important than how much you write, but you need to say enough for a reader to understand what you mean.

You will probably want to write more than a short paragraph. You should also be aware that a copy of your essay will be sent to each school that will be receiving your test results. You are to write only in the appropriate section of the answer sheet. Please write or print so that your writing may be read by someone who is not familiar with your handwriting.

You may make notes and plan your essay on the reverse side of the page. Allow enough time to copy the final form onto your answer sheet. You must copy the essay topic onto your answer sheet, in the box provided.

Please remember to write only the final draft of the essay on your answer sheet and to write it in blue or black pen. Again, you may use cursive writing or you may print. Only pages 103 and 104 will be sent to the schools.

Directions continue on the next page.

REMINDER: Please write this essay topic on the first few lines of your answer sheet.

Essay Topic

What motivational quote is your favorite and why?

- Only write on this essay question
- Only pages 103 and 104 will be sent to the schools
- Only write in blue or black pen

NOTES

_____

_____

_____

_____

_____

_____

_____

_____

_____

_____

_____

_____

_____

_____

_____

_____

_____

_____

_____

STUDENT NAME _____ GRADE APPLYING FOR _____

Use a blue or black ballpoint pen to write the final draft of your essay on this sheet.

You must write your essay topic in this space.

_____

_____

_____

Use specific details in your response

_____

_____

_____

_____

_____

_____

_____

_____

_____

_____

_____

_____

_____

_____

_____

_____

104

ISEE Middle Level Practice Tests

End of section.

If you have any time left, go over the questions in this section only.

ANSWER KEY

Verbal Reasoning

1. A	9. D	17. C	25. D	33. A
2. B	10. C	18. D	26. B	34. B
3. C	11. C	19. B	27. C	35. C
4. D	12. B	20. A	28. A	36. D
5. A	13. B	21. A	29. A	37. A
6. B	14. A	22. C	30. B	38. A
7. C	15. A	23. B	31. C	39. B
8. D	16. C	24. D	32. D	40. C

1. The correct answer is (A). Eligible means having the right to do or obtain something, satisfying the appropriate conditions or (of a person) desirable or suitable as a partner in marriage. Synonyms are desirable, competent, and worthy.

2. The correct answer is (B). Obscure means hard to make out or define; vague. Synonyms are illegible, blurry, and hazy.

3. The correct answer is (C). Drought means a prolonged period of abnormally low rainfall, leading to a shortage of water. It can also mean a prolonged absence of a specified thing. Sample: "a drought of creativity." Synonyms are dry spell, lack, and deficit.

4. The correct answer is (D). To rebuff means to reject (someone or something) in an abrupt or ungracious manner. Synonyms are to reject, refuse, and decline.

5. The correct answer is (A). Shackle refers to a pair of fetters connected by a chain, used to fasten a prisoner's wrists or ankles together. To shackle also means restrain, limit. Synonyms are to restrict, hinder, and obstruct.

6. The correct answer is (B). Stance means the attitude of a person or organization toward something, a standpoint. Synonyms are stand, opinion, and outlook.

7. The correct answer is (C). To stint means to restrict (someone) in the amount of something, especially money, given or permitted. Sample: "to avoid having to stint yourself, budget in advance." Synonyms are to limit, restrict, and budget.

8. The correct answer is (D). Derision means contemptuous ridicule or mockery. Synonyms are ridicule, mockery, and insult.

9. The correct answer is (D). To prattle is to talk at length in a foolish or inconsequential way. Synonyms are to chatter, babble, and ramble.

10. The correct answer is (C). To whet means to sharpen the blade of (a tool or weapon). It also means to excite or stimulate (someone's desire, interest, or appetite). Synonyms are to sharpen, hone, and grind.

11. The correct answer is (C). Tempest means a violent windy storm. Synonyms are storm, disturbance, and chaos.

12. The correct answer is (B). Soliloquy is an act of speaking one's thoughts aloud when by oneself or regardless of any hearers, especially by a character in a play.

13. The correct answer is (B). Middling means moderate or average in size, amount, or rank. Synonyms are average, standard, and ordinary.

14. The correct answer is (A). Meddling is a gerund from the base form meddle. To meddle means to interfere in or busy oneself unduly with something that is not one's concern. Synonyms are to interfere, intrude, and pry.

15. The correct answer is (A). Nary is nonstandard form of not. Sample: "nary a murmur or complaint"

16. The correct answer is (C). Abstruse means difficult to understand; obscure. Synonyms are puzzling, cryptic, and complicated.

17. The correct answer is (C). Athwart means across from side to side; transversely. Sample: "athwart the road was farmland as far as the eye could see"

18. The correct answer is (D). Spurious means not being what it purports to be; false or fake. Synonyms are bogus and counterfeit.

19. The correct answer is (B). To repine means to feel or express discontent, fret. Synonyms are to mourn and grieve.

20. The correct answer is (A). Adulation means obsequious flattery, excessive admiration, or praise. Synonyms are admiration, veneration, and devotion.

21. The correct answer is (A). Garrulous means excessively talkative, especially on trivial matters. In this sentence, the subject preferred silence which means she hated the excessively talkative type.

22. The correct answer is (C). Miscreant is a person who behaves badly or in a way that breaks the law. In this sentence, the police make great efforts to put the criminals behind bars.

23. The correct answer is (B). Puissant means having great power or influence. In this sentence, the subject has always wanted to be an influential man since he was a child.

24. The correct answer is (D). Riffraff means disreputable or undesirable people. It also refers to a disorganized or confused collection of things/ rubbish. In this sentence, there were piles of trash left after the music festival.

25. The correct answer is (D). To snivel means to cry and sniff in a feeble or fretful way. In this sentence, Andrea started to cry and sniff after hearing what her friend had to say.

26. The correct answer is (B). Trifling means unimportant or trivial. In this sentence, the man kept an insignificant gift in a small box which nobody noticed.

27. The correct answer is (C). Dingy means gloomy and drab. In this sentence, nobody befriended him because of his gloomy look until he changed his appearance.

28. The correct answer is (A). Chagrin means distress or embarrassment at having failed or been humiliated. In this sentence, the teacher realized to her disappointment that nobody from the class did their assignments.

29. The correct answer is (A). Fiasco refers to a thing that is a complete failure, especially in a ludicrous or humiliating way. In this sentence, the emperor's plan turned into a failure after a spy spilled the details to the enemy.

30. The correct answer is (B). To edify is to instruct or improve (someone) morally or intellectually. In this sentence, his brother's lifelong goal is to educate them with borrowed books.

31. The correct answer is (C). To lurch means to make an abrupt, unsteady, uncontrolled movement or series of movements, stagger. In this sentence, the boat violently swayed because of the strong waves.

32. The correct answer is (D). To exalt is to hold (someone or something) in very high regard; think or speak very highly of. In this sentence, the party was prepared to acclaim the kingdom's heroes of the war.

33. The correct answer is (A). To simper is to smile in an affectedly coy or ingratiating manner. In this sentence, the subject giggled behind her fan upon hearing the gentleman's words of admiration.

34. The correct answer is (B). Gaunt means (of a person) lean and haggard, especially because of suffering, hunger, or age. In this sentence, the house is haunted by a tall, skin-and-bones, woman in black.

35. The correct answer is (C). Placid means (especially of a place or stretch of water) calm and peaceful, with little movement or activity. In this sentence, never trust the calm and peaceful waters of a small lake for you never know what's hiding under.

36. The correct answer is (D). Ruddy means having a reddish color. In this sentence, the girl's cheeks turned red from embarrassment.

37. The correct answer is (A). To skulk means to move stealthily or furtively. In this sentence, the subject spent his free time loitering about the school corridors because he was shy to meet new people.

38. The correct answer is (A). To bungle means to make or do (something) in a clumsy or unskillful way. The subject was inexperienced therefore, it only made sense that she did not do well on her first attempt.

39. The correct answer is (B). To evade means to get or keep away from (as a responsibility) through cleverness or trickery. In the sentence, the subject is unable to avoid paying his dues become they have already piled up.

40. The correct answer is (C). Hearty means characterized by unqualified enthusiasm. In this sentence, the family was overjoyed to hear the pregnancy announcement.

Quantitative Reasoning

1. A	11. A	21. C	31. B
2. D	12. C	22. D	32. D
3. B	13. B	23. A	33. A
4. D	14. D	24. B	34. C
5. A	15. B	25. B	35. A
6. B	16. A	26. A	36. B
7. B	17. C	27. B	37. A
8. B	18. A	28. C	
9. D	19. D	29. B	
10. D	20. D	30. D	

1. The correct answer is (A).

   According to question

   $10 \times 5 \div 3 - 2 + 3 \Rightarrow 10 \div 5 + 3 \times 2 - 3 = 5$

2. The correct answer is (D).

$$\frac{3}{8} = \frac{3 \times 15}{8 \times 15} = \frac{45}{120} = 45$$

$$\frac{1}{4} = \frac{1 \times 30}{4 \times 30} = \frac{30}{120} = 30$$

$$\frac{5}{6} = \frac{5 \times 20}{6 \times 20} = \frac{100}{120} = 100$$

$$\frac{3}{10} = \frac{3 \times 6}{10 \times 6} = \frac{18}{120} = 18$$

As, 100 is greater than all of above values, so $\frac{3}{10}$ is the answer.

3. The correct answer is (B). 9,24,580 = 9,00,000 + 20,000 + 4,000 + 500 + 80 + 0

So, the answer is 9,00,000.

4. The correct answer is (D). $6^2 + 8^2 = 36 + 64 = 100 = 10^2$

5. The correct answer is (A). Obviously (P) × (Q) is greater than (R).

6. The correct answer is (B). The circumference of the circle = πd unit where d is the diameter, therefore circumference = 5π cm

7. The correct answer is (B). Multiplication of 97 and 57 is 5,529.

8. The correct answer is (B).

Input: Kind 12 96 heart water 59 42 yes

Step I: 12 kind 96 heat water 59 42 yes

Step II: 12 yes kind 96 heart water 59 42

Step III: 12 yes 42 kind 96 heart water 59

Step IV: 12 yes 42 water kind 96 heart 59

Step V: 12 yes 42 water 59 kind 96 heart

9. The correct answer is (D).

   Input: jungle 43 mode 25 basket 39 target 19

   Step I: 19 jungle 43 mode 25 basket 39 target

   Step II: 19 target jungle 43 mode 25 basket 39

   Step III: 19 target 25 jungle 43 mode basket 39

   Step IV: 19 target 25 mode jungle 43 basket 39

   Step V: 19 target 25 mode 39 jungle 43 basket

10. The correct answer is (D).

    It is not possible to determine the input from given step.

11. The correct answer is (A).

    Step II: 24 year 56 43 last part 64 over

    Step III: 24 year 43 56 last part 64 over

    Step IV: 24 year 43 part 56 last 64 over

    Step V: 24 year 43 part 56 over last 64

    Step VI: 24 year 43 part 56 over 64 last

    Four more steps would be required to complete the rearrangement.

12. The correct answer is (C).

    Input: 32 station 46 81 73 march go for

    Step I: 32 station 46 march 81 73 go for

    Step II: 32 station 46 march 73 81 go for

    Step III: 32 station 46 march 73 go 81 for

13. The correct answer is (B). Starting with the top left figure, one line is increasing in each figure while moving in the clockwise direction. So, four lines will come four parts.

14. The correct answer is (D).

    According to the question, total number of the candidates = 500

    Candidates failed in Math and History = 12

    Candidates failed in Math and English = 12

    Candidates failed in English and History = 10

    Candidates failed in three subjects = 5

So, the number of candidates who failed in at least two subjects

= 12 + 12 + 10 + 5 = 39

$\therefore$ Percentage = $\dfrac{39}{500} \times 100 = 7.8$

15. The correct answer is (B). $(7 \times 6 \div 2) - 6 \times 7 \div 14 = 21 - 3 = 18$.

16. The correct answer is (A).

$4x + 2 = 22$

$\Rightarrow x = 20 \div 4$

$\Rightarrow x = 5$.

$\therefore 20x + 18 = 20 \times 5 + 18 = 118$.

17. The correct answer is (C). $\dfrac{x^2}{5} + 13 = \dfrac{5^2}{5} + 13 = \dfrac{25}{5} + 13 = 5 + 13 = 8$.

18. The correct answer is (A). Half of the perimeter = $\{(60 \times 4) \div 2\}$ = 124 ft.

19. The correct answer is (D). $\sqrt[8]{256} = \sqrt[8]{2 \times 2 \times 2 \times 2 \times 2 \times 2 \times 2 \times 2} = 2$.

20. The correct answer is (D). $\dfrac{63}{7} \div \dfrac{21}{35} = \dfrac{63}{7} \times \dfrac{21}{35} = 9 \times \dfrac{3}{5} = 27 \div 5 = 5.40$.

21. The correct answer is (C). Here $x = 180° - 60° = 120°$, therefore two quantities are equal.

22. The correct answer is (D). The relationship cannot be determined from this information because we cannot find x and y individually with this information, we only have $xy = 24$.

23. The correct answer is (A). Here $\sqrt{25} + \sqrt{49} = 12$ and $\sqrt{25 + 49} = 8.602$, therefore Column A is greater.

24. The correct answer is (B). Here the area is 9, one side of the quadrilateral is 3, then the other side will be 3. Now the perimeter will be = $2 \times (3 + 3) = 12$ unit. So, Column B is greater.

25. The correct answer is (B). john had $10. He gave half of her money to his sister, so now he has = $5. Also, Jenny has now $15. So, Column B is greater.

26. The correct answer is (A). Here $2x + 5 = 63$, then $2x = 58$, so $x = 29$, and $\dfrac{y}{3} = 9$, then $y = 18$.

27. The correct answer is (B). The area of the rectangle = $3 \times 4 = 12$ sq. unit and the area of the square = 5×5 sq. unit = 25 sq. unit. Therefore, Column B is greater.

28. The correct answer is (C). The average number of chocolates = 2, and the number of chocolates eaten on Friday is 2. So, columns are equal.

29. The correct answer is (B). Here 4.9 > 0.49 therefore $\sqrt{4.9} > \sqrt{0.49}$.

30. The correct answer is (D). The relationship cannot be determined from the information which is given in this question. Here we don't know the price for one orange and one peach.

31. The correct answer is (B). Here $-(8)^6 = -1,67,77,216$ and $(-8)^6 = 1,67,77,216$, hence Column B is greater.

32. The correct answer is (D). The relationship cannot be determined from the information given. Because there are 11, 13 those are odd and A can be any one of them and there are 10, 12, 14 that are even and B can be any one of them, so it is undetermined.

33. The correct answer is (A). The prime numbers are 1, 3, 5, 7, 11 and the even numbers are 2, 4, 6, 8, 10, 12. So the probability of even number is greater than the probability of prime numbers.

34. The correct answer is (C). The fractional part of the figure that is shaded $= \dfrac{3}{20}$, hence two quantities are equal.

35. The correct answer is (A). 50% of 16 slices = 0.5 × 16 = 8 and one-fourth of the pizza = 0.25 × 16 = 4. Therefore, Column A is greater.

36. The correct answer is (B). 80% of $40 = $32 and 80% of $32 = $25.6 and 60% of $40 = $24, hence Column B is greater.

37. The correct answer is (A). The slope $= \dfrac{8-2}{5-4} = 6$ and $3x - y = -8$, then $y = 3x + 8$, therefore the slope = 3. So, Column A is greater.

Reading Comprehension and Vocabulary

1.	A	7.	B	13.	B	19.	A	25.	C	31.	B
2.	A	8.	A	14.	C	20.	C	26.	B	32.	D
3.	B	9.	A	15.	A	21.	A	27.	C	33.	A
4.	C	10.	C	16.	D	22.	D	28.	A	34.	A
5.	C	11.	B	17.	B	23.	D	29.	C	35.	D
6.	D	12.	D	18.	B	24.	B	30.	B	36.	B

1. The correct answer is (A). The passage is about how a specific breed of birds found in Japan survives storms by heading straight toward the passing typhoons and flying near the eye of the storm. This behavior is not reported in any other bird species.

2. The correct answer is (A). See line 1. The passage describes how some species of seabirds were seen with a strange behavior of flying toward the storm which might have helped them survive.

3. The correct answer is (B). See lines 27–28. The researchers attached GPS locators to 75 birds nesting on Awashima Island in Japan to track data.

4. The correct answer is (C). See lines 1–2.

5. The correct answer is (C). See lines 20–22.

6. The correct answer is (D). Veer off means to begin to go in the wrong direction.

7. The correct answer is (B). The passage talks about the story of Ninna's brain mass and how her life went after experiencing complications from the surgery. Her story was used to discuss how age can influence our response to a calamity when it strikes with young adults particularly vulnerable to getting thrown off course. See lines 34–40.

8. The correct answer is (A). The passage talks about the story of Ninna's brain mass and how her life went after experiencing complications from the surgery. Her story was used to discuss how age can influence our response to a calamity when it strikes with young adults particularly vulnerable to getting thrown off course. See lines 34–40.

9. The correct answer is (A). See lines 2–3.

10. The correct answer is (C). See lines 24–26.

11. The correct answer is (B). See lines 36–40.

12. The correct answer is (D). Being unmoored means being (of a person) insecure, confused, or lacking contact with reality.

13. The correct answer is (B). See lines 20–30. The passage talked about cable bacteria from Chesapeake Bay mud and how the bacteria have been removing toxic sulfides and prevent them from moving up the water column which may protect fish, crustaceans, and other aquatic organisms from a "toxic nightmare."

14. The correct answer is (C). See lines 13–15.

15. The correct answer is (A). See lines 17–30.

16. The correct answer is (D). See lines 27–30.

17. The correct answer is (B). Clad is the past participle of "clothe." Synonyms are dressed and wearing.

18. The correct answer is (B). Hauled is the past tense of "haul." To haul means to pull or drag with effort or force.

19. The correct answer is (A). The passage talked about the studies on how wolves that bred with black coats helped them survive measles like virus in the North America and how their black coat played a role in their immune systems.

20. The correct answer is (C). See lines 1–2.

21. The correct answer is (A). See lines 2–9, lines 20–22.

22. The correct answer is (D). Tryst means a private romantic rendezvous between lovers.

23. The correct answer is (D). In the sentence, fundamental is used as an adjective which means forming a necessary base or core, of central importance.

24. The correct answer is (B). To scoff means to treat or address with derision, mock.

25. The correct answer is (C). The passage talked about the new study showing that we can protect fish and eat more of them, too. See lines 11–12.

26. The correct answer is (B). See lines 8–10. Hawaii is a constituent state of the United States of America.

27. The correct answer is (C). See lines 27–30.

28. The correct answer is (A). See lines 11–12.

29. The correct answer is (C). In this sentence, "reserves" is used as a noun which means a protected area for wildlife.

30. The correct answer is (B). Prohibited means that has been forbidden; banned.

31. The correct answer is (B). The passage discussed how it was concluded in the study that dogs can detect odor associated with humans' response to stress. See lines 30–33.

32. The correct answer is (D). See lines 30–33.

33. The correct answer is (A). See lines 2–3.

34. The correct answer is (A). See lines 4–8.

35. The correct answer is (D). See lines 33–37.

36. The correct answer is (B). Volatile means (of a substance) easily evaporated at normal temperatures. In this passage it refers to the substance used in the research which was samples of breath and sweat.

Mathematics Achievement

1. B	11. B	21. B	31. B	41. C
2. D	12. B	22. D	32. A	42. A
3. C	13. D	23. C	33. D	43. B
4. C	14. A	24. A	34. B	44. D
5. C	15. D	25. B	35. A	45. B
6. C	16. C	26. D	36. A	46. C
7. A	17. D	27. D	37. B	47. A
8. D	18. D	28. C	38. A	
9. A	19. A	29. D	39. C	
10. A	20. C	30. C	40. D	

1. The correct answer is (B).

Let, selling price of 20 books is $20

So, selling price of 4 books is $4

∴ Purchasing price = 26 – 4 = $16

∴ Profit = $4

∴ Percentage of Profit = $\left(\dfrac{4 \times 100}{16}\right)\% = 25\%$

2. The correct answer is (D).

   $(18 \times 45 + 7 \times 48) = 1,146$

   Average per kg price $= \dfrac{1,146}{25} = 45.84$.

3. The correct answer is (C).

   $r = +, s = \div, t = -, u = \times$

   $9\ r\ 2\ s\ 10\ t\ 7\ u\ 21 = 9 + 2 \div 10 - 7 \times 21 = -137.80$

4. The correct answer is (C).

   $1,510.04 - 118 \div 81 + 64 = 1,572.58$

5. The correct answer is (C).

   $118 \div 11.5 = 10.26$

6. The correct answer is (C).

   $3 - 11 + 3 = -5;\ 5 - 11 + 3 = -3;\ 9 - 11 + 3 = 1;\ 11 - 11 + 3 = 3;\ 13 - 11 + 3 = \underline{5}$.

7. The correct answer is (A).

   $120 \div 12 = 10 \Rightarrow 1 - 9 \Rightarrow 2 + 8 \Rightarrow 3 + 7 \Rightarrow 4 + 6 \Rightarrow 5 + 5$

   Here, $(1, 9)$ and $(3, 7)$ are mutually prime

   $\therefore$ There are two pairs.

8. The correct answer is (D).

   $15,000 + 21,588 \div x = 20,397$

   $\Rightarrow \dfrac{21,588}{x} = 20,397\ \ 15,000$

   $\Rightarrow \dfrac{21,588}{x} = 5,397$

   $\Rightarrow x = 21,588 \div 5,397 = 4$

9. The correct answer is (A).

$$\sqrt{8} = \sqrt{4 \times 2} = 2\sqrt{2} = 2 \times 1.414 = 2.828$$

$$\frac{17}{6} = 2.833....$$

$$\frac{82}{29} = 2.822....$$

$$\therefore \frac{82}{29}, \sqrt{8}, \frac{17}{6}$$

10. The correct answer is (A).

Let, $0.98 = a$ and $0.1 = b$

$$\therefore \frac{(a)^3 - (b)^3}{(a)^2 + (ab) + (b)^2} = \frac{(a-b)(a^2 + ab + b^2)}{(a^2 + ab + b^2)} = a - b = 0.98 - 0.10 = 0.88$$

11. The correct answer is (B).

We know the total value of all angles of a triangle is 180°.

So, 180° – (90° + 27°) = 63°.

12. The correct answer is (B).

As, $(a + b)^3 = a^3 + 3a^2b + 3ab^2 + b^3$,

So, $(n + o)^3 = n^3 + 3n^2o + 3no^2 + o^3$

13. The correct answer is (D).

$3^8 - 3^5 = 6,561 - 243 = 3,618$.

14. The correct answer is (A).

$$\frac{8 + 3 + 13}{6} = 4,$$

$$\frac{10 + 5 + 15}{6} = 5,$$

$$\therefore ? = \frac{21 + 10 + 11}{6} = 7.$$

15. The correct answer is (D).

Number of events in Hall C $\Rightarrow$ 210 – 35 = 175

Number of events in Hall D $\Rightarrow$ 280 – 55 = 225

$\therefore$ Required ratio = 175:225 = 7:9

16. The correct answer is (C).

Number of events in Hall E $\Rightarrow$ 265 – 25 = 240

$\therefore$ Non-marriage reception events $\Rightarrow \dfrac{240 \times 15}{100} = 36$

Number of events in Hall A $\Rightarrow$ 242 – 32 = 210

$\therefore$ Non-marriage reception events $\Rightarrow \dfrac{210 \times 20}{100} = 42 = 42$

$\Rightarrow$ Required percent

$\Rightarrow \left(\dfrac{42 - 36}{42} \right) \times 100 = 14\dfrac{2}{7}$

17. The correct answer is (D).

Number of events in Hall B in 2016 $\Rightarrow$ 254 – 30 = 224

$\therefore$ Number of events held in 2018 $= 224 \times \dfrac{9}{8} = 22$

Number of events cancelled in 2018 $= \dfrac{30 \times 120}{100} = 36$

$\therefore$ Number of events booked = 252 + 36 = 288

18. The correct answer is (D).

Number of marriage receptions held:

Hall A $\Rightarrow \dfrac{210 \times 80}{100} = 168$

Hall B $\Rightarrow \dfrac{224 \times 75}{200} = 168$

Hall D $\Rightarrow \dfrac{225 \times 80}{100} = 180$

$\therefore$ Required average $= \dfrac{168 + 168 + 180}{3} = 172$

19. The correct answer is (A).

Required difference = (210 + 240) – (32 + 25) = 450 – 57 = 393

20. The correct answer is (C).

    Ratio of the shares of A, B, and C = Ratio of the equivalent capitals of A, B, and C for one month

    = $4,000 \times 12 : 4,500 \times 6 : 6,000 \times 3 = 16 : 9 : 6$

    The sum of the terms of ratio = $16 + 9 + 6 = 31$

    If total annual profit be x.

    Then B's share = $\$\dfrac{9x}{31}$

    $\therefore \dfrac{9x}{31} = 18,000$

    $\Rightarrow x = \dfrac{18,000 \times 31}{9} = \$62,000.$

21. The correct answer is (B).

    Percentage of students playing both = $(50 + 40 + 18) - 100 = 8\%$

22. The correct answer is (D). H.C.F. of 51, 68, and 85 is 17.

23. The correct answer is (C). $\dfrac{352 \times 21 \times 20 \times 21}{21 \times 21 \times 20} = 352$

24. The correct answer is (A). $209.44 \div 4 = 52.36.$

25. The correct answer is (B).

    $19^3 = 19 \times 19 \times 19 = 6,859.$

26. The correct answer is (D). $45 \div 0.59 = 76.27.$

27. The correct answer is (D). L.C.M. of 34, 68, and 102 is 204.

28. The correct answer is (C).

    $x = 18$ and $y = 9$

    So, $2x^2 + 3y = (2 \times 18^2) + (3 \times 9) = (2 \times 324) + 29 = 648 + 29 = 677.$

29. The correct answer is (D).

    $875 \div 25 = 35$

    $254 - 35 = 219$

30. The correct answer is (C).

$$\frac{2}{5}\% = \frac{2}{5 \times 100} = \frac{2}{500} = \frac{1}{250}.$$

31. The correct answer is (B).

Let, after covering x km both train meet

So, $\dfrac{x}{60} = \dfrac{x}{75} + \dfrac{1}{2}$

or, $\dfrac{x}{60} = \dfrac{2x + 75}{150}$

or, $\dfrac{x}{2} = \dfrac{2x + 75}{150}$

$\therefore 5x = 4x + 150$

$\therefore x = 150$

So, distance is 150 km.

32. The correct answer is (A).

$\dfrac{x}{x+1} = \dfrac{4}{5} \Rightarrow 5x = 4x + 4 \Rightarrow x = 4$

33. The correct answer is (D).

$9 \times 1 = 9, 9 \times 9 = 81$

Similarly, $8 \times 1 = 8, 8 \times 8 = 64$.

34. The correct answer is (B).

$s = 631.25$ and $t = 31.17$

So, $s/t = 631.25/31.17 = 20.25$ (approx.).

35. The correct answer is (A).

$\dfrac{9.5 \times 0.85}{0.0017 \times 0.19} = 902.5.$

36. The correct answer is (A).

$462 - 42 = 420$

$420 - 42 = 378$

$378 - 42 = 336$

$336 - 42 = 294$

So, the number 370 is wrong in this series.

37. The correct answer is (B).

$$\text{L.C.M.} = \frac{1{,}863}{27} = 69$$

So, numbers are 69 and 27 which satisfy the given condition

Hence the other no. = 69.

38. The correct answer is (A).

$$\sin^2\theta + \sin\theta = 1$$

$$\Rightarrow \sin\theta = 1 - \sin^2\theta = \cos^2\theta$$

$$\cos^4\theta + \cos^2\theta = (\cos^2\theta)^2 + \cos^2\theta = \sin^2\theta + \cos^2\theta = 1.$$

39. The correct answer is (C).

Let the sum = x

$$\therefore 1{,}352 = x\left(1 + \frac{4}{100}\right)^2$$

$$\text{or, } 1{,}352 = x\left(\frac{26}{25}\right)^2$$

$$\text{or, } x = \frac{1{,}352 \times 25{,}125}{26 \times 26}$$

or, $x = \$1{,}250$.

40. The correct answer is (D).

As per rules $\left[x + y + \dfrac{xy}{100}\right]$

$$\Rightarrow -10 - 20 + \frac{(-10 \times -20)}{100} = -30 + 2 = 28\%$$

41. The correct answer is (C).

1,224 is divisible by 6, 12, and 17.

42. The correct answer is (A).

$$\frac{5}{6} \times \frac{36}{45} = \frac{2}{3}$$

43. The correct answer is (B).

Perimeter of one face, $4a = 32$ cm

Side of a cube = $a = 8$ cm

$\therefore$ Volume of cube = $a^3 = (8)^3 = 512$ cm^3

44. The correct answer is (D).

$$\frac{5}{13}x = 12 + 2y$$

$$\Rightarrow 5x = 156 + 26y$$

$$\Rightarrow 5x - 26y = 156.$$

45. The correct answer is (B).

$$a^2 + b^2 = 2ab \Rightarrow (a - b)^2 = 0$$

$$(a - b)^2 = (a + b)^2 + 4ab = 4ab.$$

46. The correct answer is (C).

S.P. of an article = 20% and 15%

Successive discount × marked price of an article

or, $3,060 = \dfrac{80}{100} \times \dfrac{85}{100} \times$ Marked Price

Marked price of an article $= \dfrac{3,060 \times 100 \times 100}{80 \times 85} = \$4,500.$

47. The correct answer is (A).

$45 \times 4 - (40 \div 4) + 11 (3 + 7) = 180 - 10 + 11 \times 10 = 180 - 10 + 110 = 280.$

$\therefore 280$ is divisible by 14.

Sample Essay Response

There are too many motivational quotes to mention. You can pick one motivational quote for every day you feel demotivated, need an inspiration or when you need to get yourself out of procrastination. You can get a different motivational quote for every stage of life you're in. You get them from anyone and sometimes not all of them leave a significant impact in your life.

My favorite motivational quote has been, "If you ever feel like giving up, just look back on how far you've come already." This quote has stuck with me through the years I have spent building my career and it has helped me through the times it felt difficult to keep going. I can't remember where I heard or saw it from, but I took it by heart.

My family is not rich. I went to public schools and depended on scholarships through my college. I grew up with the burden of being the eldest. There was no other way for me but to excel academically so I can afford to go to college and hopefully support my siblings when I graduate. Every waking hour was an opportunity to me to better myself and move a step closer to my goal. There was little time to spare for play and fun. At a young age, I had already realized that life is hard and nobody else will save you but yourself.

Fast forward to where I am now, I can say I am successful. I have a stable income, have advanced my career and supporting my younger sister through college. She will be graduating soon and looking back to the past years is both exhilarating and exhausting. It is not always butterflies and rainbows. Hurricanes come and life happens. I have learned to accept that you will not always be on top because somebody else needs to have their shot too. There will be times you won't feel the same enthusiasm towards your goal, and I believe that's okay. You will feel tired but what I always keep in mind is when you feel tired, giving up is not the solution. When you feel tired, then it's time to take a pause, rest and reflect. Then, I always look back to my favorite motivational quote, "If you ever feel like giving up, just look back on how far you've come already."

I still have more goals to accomplish for myself and for my future family. This motivational quote will keep me going as it always been.

For the ISEE, the most commonly referenced score is the stanine score. Check out the four steps to calculating stanine scores.

Step 1: The Raw Score

The first step in scoring is calculating a raw score. This is quite simple.

Students receive one point for each correct answer and no points for incorrect answers or unanswered questions.

Tip: Because there is no score penalty for incorrect answers or unanswered questions, be sure to answer every single question! Answering all of the questions can only increase your chances of a higher score.

Step 2: The Scaled Score

Once a raw score has been calculated for each section, it is converted into a scaled score.

This conversion adjusts for the variation in difficulty between different tests. Thus, a lower raw score on a harder test could give you the same scaled score as a higher raw score on an easier test. This process is called equating.

The scaled score for each section ranges from 760 to 940.

Step 3: The Percentile Score

Next, the percentile score for each section is calculated.

Percentiles compare a student's scaled score to all other same-grade students from the past three years. This is important to understand because the ISEE is taken by students in a range of grades. The Upper Level ISEE, for instance, is taken by students applying to grades 9–12; however, the percentile score is based only on the performance of other students applying to the same grade. Thus, a student applying to 9th grade will not be compared to a student applying to 12th grade.

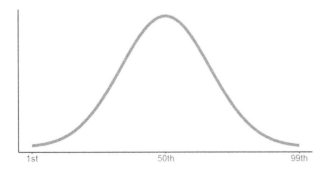

Here's an example to help understand percentile scores: scoring in the 40th percentile indicates that a student scored the same or higher than 40% of students in the same grade but lower than 59% of students.

Step 4: The Stanine Score

Finally, the percentile is converted into a stanine score.

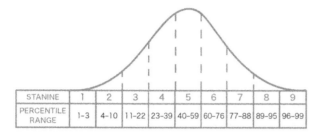

STANINE	1	2	3	4	5	6	7	8	9
PERCENTILE RANGE	1–3	4–10	11–22	23–39	40–59	60–76	77–88	89–95	96–99

Notice that the percentile ranges for the middle stanines of 4–6 are far larger than the ranges for the extreme stanines of 1, 2, 8, or 9. This means that most students taking the ISEE achieve scores in the middle ranges. Only the top 4% of all test takers receive a stanine of 9 on any given section, while 20% of students receive a stanine of 5.

So, what is a good ISEE score?

Stanine scores (which range from 1 to 9) are the most important and are the scores schools pay the most attention to. But what is a good score on the ISEE? A score of 5 or higher will be enough to put students in the running for most schools, although some elite private schools want applicants to have ISEE test results of 7 or higher.

Here's a sample ISEE Report

Individual Student Report

Candidate for Grade	**8**
ID Number	
Gender	**Male**
Date of Birth	**4/8/2004**
Phone Number	
Test Level/Form	**Middle/0916**
Date of Testing	**11/30/2016**
Tracking Number	**201612010592103**

The Test Profile below shows your total scores for each test. Refer to the enclosed brochure called *Understanding the Individual Student Report* to help you interpret the *Test Profile* and *Analysis*. Percentile Ranks and Stanines are derived from norms for applicants to independent schools.

TEST PROFILE

Section	Scaled Score (760 – 940)	Percentile Rank (1 – 99)	Stanine (1 – 9)	Stanine Analysis 1 2 3 4 5 6 7 8 9
Verbal Reasoning	895	90	8	V
Reading Comprehension	890	76	6	R
Quantitative Reasoning	894	81	7	Q
Mathematics Achievement	883	61	6	M

LEGEND: V = Verbal Reasoning R = Reading Comprehension Q = Quantitative Reasoning M = Mathematics Achievement

ANALYSIS

Section & Subsection	# of Questions	# Correct	Results for Each Question
Verbal Reasoning			
Synonyms	18	15	++++++++- ++++- ++- +
Single Word Response	17	16	+++++++++++- +++++
Quantitative Reasoning			
Word Problems	18	11	+++- - - +++- +++++- - -
Quantitative Comparisons	14	14	++++++++++++++
Reading Comprehension			
Main Idea	4	4	++++
Supporting Ideas	6	5	- +++++
Inference	6	5	+- ++++
Vocabulary	7	5	+++- +- +
Organization/Logic	4	4	++++
Tone/Style/Figurative Language	3	3	+++
Mathematics Achievement			
Whole Numbers	7	4	+- +++- -
Decimals, Percents, Fractions	9	5	++- - ++- - +
Algebraic Concepts	11	7	+++++- ++- - -
Geometry	4	2	+- +-
Measurement	5	4	++++-
Data Analysis and Probability	6	4	+++- +-

LEGEND: + = Correct   - = Incorrect   S = Skipped   N = Not Reached

The test was administered in the order reported in the analysis section; Verbal Reasoning, Quantitative Reasoning, Reading Comprehension, and Mathematics Achievement. Each section was divided into subsections, grouping similar types of questions. The Reading Comprehension subsection grouping does not represent the actual order of the test questions.

The above is a preliminary ISEE report. ERB reserves the right to amend this report before it is finalized. The report will be final no later than 20 business days. The final report will automatically be generated electronically.

ISEE—Middle Level Exam-3

Verbal Reasoning

You have 20 minutes to answer the 40 questions in the Verbal Reasoning Section.

This section is divided into two parts that contain two different types of questions. As soon as you have completed Part I, answer the questions in Part II. You may write in your test booklet. For each answer you select, fill in the corresponding circle on your answer document.

Part I—Synonyms

Each question in Part I consists of a word in capital letters followed by four answer choices. Select the one word that is most nearly the same in meaning as the word in capital letters.

SAMPLE QUESTION:	<u>Sample Answer</u>
CHARGE:	A B ● D
(A) release	
(B) belittle	
(C) accuse	
(D) conspire	

Part II—Sentence Completion

Each question in Part II is made up of a sentence with one blank. Each blank indicates that a word or phrase is missing. The sentence is followed by four answer choices. Select the word or phrase that will best complete the meaning of the sentence as a whole.

SAMPLE QUESTIONS:	<u>Sample Answer</u>
It rained so much that the streets were _____.	● B C D
(A) flooded	
(B) arid	
(C) paved	
(D) crowded	
The house was so dirty that it took _____.	A B C ●
(A) less than 10 min to wash it	
(B) four months to demolish it	
(C) over a week to walk across it	
(D) two days to clean it	

133

Part I—Synonyms

Directions:

Select the word that is most nearly the same in meaning as the word in capital letters.

1. FLAIR

   (A) style (B) flicker (C) stare (D) flash

2. FERRET

   (A) bird (B) overlook (C) explore (D) miss

3. GINGERLY

   (A) bold (B) cautious (C) yellowish (D) reckless

4. GLUT

   (A) scarcity (B) excess (C) intestines (D) diet

5. GRAPPLE

   (A) avoid (B) fruit (C) release (D) struggle

6. INAUGURATE

   (A) end (B) terminate (C) annul (D) launch

7. VIE

   (A) purchase (B) compete (C) see (D) concede

8. VORACIOUS

   (A) greedy (B) satiated (C) content (D) full

9. CYNIC

   (A) pessimist (B) optimist (C) fan (D) supporter

10. DEBILITATING

(A) interesting   (B) engaging   (C) exhausting   (D) inspiring

11. DEARTH

(A) surplus   (B) shortage   (C) abundance   (D) soil

12. FEIGN

(A) sincere   (B) unconscious   (C) genuine   (D) fake

13. GIST

(A) visitor   (B) essence   (C) surface   (D) lie

14. CONNOISSEUR

(A) butler   (B) receptionist   (C) expert   (D) amateur

15. LOATH

(A) hesitant   (B) willing   (C) eager   (D) glad

16. ABASE

(A) honor   (B) celebrate   (C) praise   (D) degrade

17. ABSCOND

(A) dwell   (B) escape   (C) stay   (D) return

18. ABATE

(A) intensify   (B) subside   (C) rise   (D) escalate

19. ACCEDE

(A) agree   (B) reject   (C) refuse   (D) deny

20. ABJECT

(A) arrogant   (B) superior   (C) humble   (D) proud

Part II—Sentence Completion

> **Directions:**
>
> Select the word that best completes the sentence.

21. The rain was a blessing in _____ because the test got cancelled.

    (A) disguise (B) apparition (C) reflection (D) shadow

22. William's parents will be cutting him some _____ because he worked hard last year.

    (A) allowance (B) play (C) opinion (D) slack

23. Her curfew is _____ after getting the highest marks on the exams.

    (A) lengthened (B) extended (C) prolonged (D) abridged

24. Reporters _____ her one time while walking her dog so she stays at home.

    (A) avoided (B) accosted (C) evaded (D) dodged

25. Father was _____ when he heard of my teenage sister's pregnancy.

    (A) unperturbed (B) adventurous (C) aghast (D) bold

26. Your donations will _____ many children's hunger.

    (A) impair (B) allay (C) aggravate (D) exacerbate

27. A riverside _____ with a loved one may help ease your anxiety.

    (A) amble (B) argument (C) battle (D) party

28. Billy looked with _____ eyes at his bullies as he finally stood up for himself.

    (A) friendly (B) bright (C) baleful (D) innocent

29. The waitress reported a _____ guest who initiated a fight with the next table for ignoring his remarks.

    (A) friendly (B) neutral (C) belligerent (D) bored

30. The neighbor got arrested for _____ money by passing fake solicitation envelopes to unsuspecting elderly.

    (A) publishing (B) bilking (C) giving (D) handing

31. Chris asked for a paternity test to present as a _____ evidence that he's the father of the child.

    (A) irrelevant (B) cogent (C) invalid (D) weak

32. Unknowingly, a _____ is brewing with the drug traffickers and the armed forces behind Sergeant Claire's back.

    (A) disagreement (B) fight (C) conflict (D) collusion

33. Alice's _____ artistry won numerous awards all over the globe.

    (A) deft (B) crude (C) amateur (D) inept

34. The war left the cities _____.

    (A) derelict (B) restored (C) salvaged (D) reclaimed

35. The sudden break up left her _____ for months.

    (A) hopeful (B) cheerful (C) optimistic (D) despondent

36. With his hands raised, he _____ his triumphant return from the war.

    (A) criticized (B) extolled (C) punished (D) blamed

37. She was warned to not trust him because he is a known _____.

    (A) fabulist (B) expert (C) friend (D) figure

38. The team went on vacation _____ their success on their latest project after facing several crises.

    (A) exulting (B) grieving (C) regretting (D) bemoaning

39. The movie's villain had a grand scheme to _____ the main character in failing his quest therefore winning the king's favor for himself.

    (A) discourage (B) abet (C) tame (D) hold

40. He committed such an _____ crime nobody dares to remember.

    (A) delightful (B) appealing (C) enjoyable (D) atrocious

End of section.

If you have any time left, go over the questions in this section only.

Do not start the next section.

You have 35 minutes to answer the 37 questions in the Quantitative Reasoning Section.

Each question is followed by four suggested answers. Read each question and then decide which one of the four suggested answers is best.

Find the row of spaces on your document that has the same number as the question. In this row, mark the space having the same letter as the answer you have chosen. You may write in your test booklet.

EXAMPLE 1:

What is the value of the expression $(4 + 6) \div 2$?

(A) 2
(B) 4
(C) 5
(D) 7

<u>Sample Answer</u>

A   B   ●   D

The correct answer is 5, so circle C is darkened.

EXAMPLE 2:

A square has an area of 25 cm². What is the length of one of its side?

(A) 1 cm
(B) 5 cm
(C) 10 cm
(D) 25 cm

A   ●   C   D

The correct answer is 5 cm, so circle B is darkened.

---

1. If "+" means "minus," "−" means "multiply," "÷" means "plus," and "×" means "divide," then; $20 \times 4 \div 3 - 2 + 1 = ?$

   (A) 10   (B) $\dfrac{53}{5}$ (C) 21   (D) 36

2. What is the smallest value among these?

   $\dfrac{3}{2}, \dfrac{1}{8}, \dfrac{4}{6}, \dfrac{2}{10}$

   (A) $\dfrac{3}{2}$ (B) $\dfrac{2}{10}$ (C) $\dfrac{4}{6}$ (D) $\dfrac{1}{8}$

3. What is the value of the digit 2 in the number 9,24,580?

   (A) 0.20,000   (B) 2,00,000   (C) 20,000   (D) 2.00000

4. $3^2 + 4^2 =$

   (A) 5^2 (B) 6^2 (C) 14^2 (D) 15^2

5. Examine the best answer.

   (P) 5^3

   (Q) 3^5

   (R) $5^3 \times 3^5$

   (A) (P) × (Q) is greater than (R)   (B) (P) − (Q) is an irrational number

   (C) (Q) is the greatest number   (D) none of these

6. Find circumference of the circle whose diameter is 10 cm.

   (A) 10π cm   (B) 5π cm   (C) 25π cm   (D) 50π cm

7. $103 \times 97 =$

   (A) 9,991   (B) 10,397   (C) 6,012   (D) 5,782

Questions 8–12

Study the following information carefully and answer the following questions given below.

In these series, you will be looking at both the letter pattern and the number pattern. Fill the blank in the middle of the series or end of the series.

8. Input: SCD, TEF, UGH, _____, WKL

    (A) CMN (B) UJI (C) VIJ (D) IJT

9. Input: B_2CD, _____, BCD_4, B_5CD, BC_6D

    (A) B_2C_2D (B) BC_3D (C) B_2C_3D (D) none of the above

10. Input: FAG, GAF, HAI, IAH, _____

    (A) JAK (B) HAL (C) HAK (D) JAI

11. Input: ELFA, GLHA, ILJA, _____, MLNA

    (A) OLPA (B) KLMA (C) LLMA (D) KLLA

12. Input: CMM, EOO, GQQ, _____, KUU

    (A) GRR (B) GSS (C) ISS (D) ITT

13. Find the correct one.

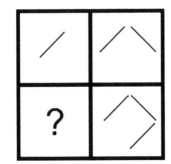

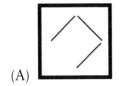 (A)   (B)   (C)   (D)

14. Consider the following Venn diagram.

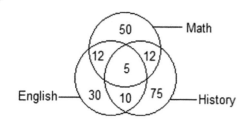

Five hundred candidates appeared in an examination comprising of tests in English, Mathematics, and History. The diagram gives the number of the candidates who failed in different tests. What is the percentage of the candidates who failed in at least three subjects?

(A) 1%   (B) 5%   (C) 6.8%   (D) 7.8%

15. $(8 \times 15 \div 5) - 16 \times 3 \div 8 =$

(A) 100   (B) 18   (C) –15   (D) 8

16. If $4x + 2 = 22$, then what is the value of $20x + 50$?

(A) 118   (B) 150   (C) 132   (D) 140

17. If $x = 2$; then find the value of $\dfrac{x^2}{5} + 12$

(A) $\dfrac{64}{5}$ (B) $\dfrac{9}{5}$ (C) $\dfrac{18}{5}$ (D) $\dfrac{26}{5}$

18. What is the half of the perimeter of a square with a side of 30 ft?

(A) 60 ft   (B) 150 sq. ft   (C) 130 ft   (D) 180 ft

19. $\sqrt[4]{625} = ?$

(A) 128   (B) 85   (C) 5   (D) 2

20. $\dfrac{64}{7} \div \dfrac{8}{49} =$

(A) 60   (B) 56   (C) 28   (D) 50

Directions:

Using all information given in each question, compare the quantity in Column A to the quantity in Column B. All questions in Part II have these answers choice:

(A) the quantity in Column A is greater

(B) the quantity in Column B is greater

(C) the two quantities are equal

(D) the relationship cannot be determined from the information given

21.

70   x

Column A	Column B
x	130

22. A rectangle with sides x and y has an area of 56.

Column A	Column B
The length of x	The length of y

23.

Column A	Column B
$\sqrt{64} + \sqrt{25}$	$\sqrt{25 + 64}$

24.

A B

4

D C

The quadrilateral $ABCD$ has an area of 16.

Column A	Column B
The perimeter of $ABCD$	12

143

25. John had $20. He gave half of her money to her sister, Jenny. Jenny now has $30.

Column A	Column B
The amount of money John now has	The amount of money Jenny had originally

26. $2x + 3 = 13$

$\dfrac{y}{2} + 6 = 8$

Column A	Column B
x	y

27.

Column A	Column B
The area of a rectangle with length 10 and width 5	The area of a square with a side of 8

28. **Number of Chocolates Eaten Each Day**

Wednesday	5
Thursday	6
Friday	3
Saturday	2

Column A	Column B
The average number of chocolates eaten each day	The number of chocolates eaten on Friday

29.

Column A	Column B
$\sqrt{1.00}$	$\sqrt{100}$

30. Amy bought 5 oranges and 12 peaches. The total price of the fruit was $3.80.

Column A	Column B
The cost of one orange	The cost of one peach

31.

Column A	Column B
$-(2)^5$	$(-2)^5$

32. A represents an odd integer greater than 9 and less than 13.
B represents an even integer greater than 10 and less than 13.

Column A	Column B
A	B

33. A six-sided die with faces numbered 1–6 is rolled.

Column A	Column B
The probability that the result is even	The probability that the result is prime

34.

Column A	Column B
The fractional part of the figure that is shaded	$\dfrac{4}{20}$

35. Melvin brought a large pizza with 20 slices.

Column A	Column B
The number of slices left if Melvin eats 50% of the pizza	The number of slices left if Melvin eats one-fourth of the pizza

36. The original price of a phone case that is now on sale was $100.

Column A	Column B
The price of the case after two 20% discount	The price of the case after a single 40% discount

37.

Column A	Column B
The slope of the line with points (4,2) and (8, 10)	The slope of the line $2x - y = -18$

End of section.

If you have any time left, go over the questions in this section only.

Do not start the next section.

You have 25 minutes to answer the 36 questions in the Reading Comprehension and Vocabulary section.

Directions:

This section contains six short reading passages. Each passage is followed by six questions based on its content. Answer the questions following each passage on the basis of what is stated or implied in that passage. You may write in your test booklet.

Questions 1–6

Even before their daughter was born in June, Aaron and Helen Chavez knew she would need heart surgery. Doctors expected her to have an operation around 6 months of age.

When it became apparent in September that it would have to happen much sooner than expected, the Chavezes said, they endured an agonizing monthlong wait for a bed to open at their local children's hospital so baby MJ could have the procedure she needed.

"They said, 'Well, we would love to get her in as soon as possible. However, right now, we don't have beds,'" Aaron said.

Space for children in hospitals is at a premium across the country. Data reported to the US government shows that as of Friday, more than three-quarters of pediatric hospital beds and 80% of intensive care beds for kids are full. That's up from an average of about two-thirds full over the past two years.

Federal data shows that the strain on hospital beds for kids began in August and September, which is right around the start of the school year in many areas.

Hospitals are seeing higher than normal numbers of sick infants and children due to a particularly early and severe season for respiratory infections in kids, including respiratory syncytial virus, or RSV, and influenza.

As of Friday, Golisano Children's Hospital in Rochester, New York, the facility that treated the Chavezes' daughter, was over capacity. Federal data shows that it has been consistently more full than the national average over the past few months. Golisano went from having 85% of its beds occupied in August to over 100% now.

1. The main objective of this passage is

   (A) to inform readers how prevalent hospital shortages are

   (B) to persuade people to not go to the hospital because they are full

   (C) to invite people to donate for Chavezes' daughter

   (D) to scare people from contracting any illness because of hospital shortages

2. What procedure did the Chavezes' daughter needed?

   (A) brain surgery   (B) heart surgery   (C) colon surgery   (D) cleft lip surgery

3. When did the strain on hospital bed start?

   (A) January and February   (B) March and April

   (C) August and September   (D) October and November

4. Why are there shortages for pediatric beds?

   (A) hospitals are undergoing renovation

   (B) hospitals are filing for bankruptcy

   (C) hospitals are replacing their beds and delivery is delayed

   (D) hospitals are seeing higher than normal numbers of sick infants and children

5. What does the underlined word in line 8 mean?

   (A) unbearable   (B) gratifying   (C) acceptable   (D) tolerable

6. What does the underlined phrase in line 14 mean?

   (A) scarce and in demand   (B) with additional charge   (C) luxurious   (D) high-end

Questions 7–12

Actress Christina Applegate apparently overlooked the early symptoms of multiple sclerosis (MS) before she was diagnosed last summer while on the set of the third and final season of "Dead To Me," which will drop on Netflix Nov. 17.

"I got diagnosed while we were working," the Emmy winner recently told Variety during an interview.

"I had to call everybody and be like, 'I have multiple sclerosis, guys.'"

She added, "And then it was about kind of learning—all of us learning—what I was going to be capable of doing."

She is opening up about her early signs and symptoms of MS.

One common early symptom includes difficulty with vision, such as blurry vision or even blindness in one eye, the same source added.

Most patients also experience muscle weakness in their arms or legs and difficulty with balance that can become so severe they have trouble walking or standing.

"MS can present with isolated eye vision loss, numbness, tingling in your face [and] double vision, usually lasting for days and not hours or minutes," said Dr. Michael G. Ho, assistant clinical professor of neurology at UCLA in California.

But these symptoms are nonspecific and subtle, so they can be initially dismissed by patients.

"Approximately half of all people with MS experience cognitive impairments such as difficulties with concentration, attention, memory and poor judgment, but such symptoms are usually mild and are frequently overlooked," according to the National Institute of Neurological Disorders and Stroke's website.

"Sometimes when the symptoms are mild and people fully recover, they might decide not to see a doctor because they attributed it to any number of causes, including 'pinched nerve,' stress, etc.," Perumal told Fox News Digital.

7. The key point of the passage is

   (A) to share that Christina Applegate is diagnosed with MS

   (B) to educate readers how MS symptoms are often overlooked

   (C) to promote Christina Applegate's upcoming show

   (D) to advertise Netflix

8. What health condition is the topic of the passage?

   (A) multiple sores   (B) multiple scabies   (C) multiple sclerosis   (D) multiple sickle cell disease

9. Why are MS symptoms often overlooked?

   (A) because there are no early signs and symptoms

   (B) because there is no modern technology to diagnose early stage of MS

   (C) because patients do not see their doctors

   (D) because symptoms are nonspecific and subtle which are often attributed to number of causes, including 'pinched nerve,' stress, etc.

10. Which among the symptoms below is not a mentioned symptom of MS in the passage?

    (A) vomiting   (B) muscle weakness   (C) vision loss   (D) tingling in the face

11. What does the underlined word in line 2 mean?

    (A) notice   (B) miss   (C) spot   (D) face

12. In line 41, what does the underlined word mean?

    (A) honor   (B) disregard   (C) blame   (D) discredit

Questions 13–18

Derrick Morgan moved to Mexico during the pandemic after a solo trip.

"I fell in love with the culture, the people, just everything about the city," the 31-year-old attorney and self-described "digital nomad" said.

The warm weather and relaxed Covid restrictions played a part in his decision to spend more time there after he first visited at the end of 2019. He now lives and works in Mexico City during the fall and the winter—he calls himself a "snowbird"—and he stays in short-term rental properties. The most enticing factor? It's less expensive to live there than when he's at his Chicago condominium.

"I was living in an apartment that was just as nice as my condo but for a third of the price. You can't really beat that," Morgan said, noting Mexico's cost of living in general was almost half of what it is stateside.

Mexico City has seen an influx of people migrating to the historic metropolis, especially during the pandemic when remote work made it possible to work from different places. Currently, 1.6 million Americans live in Mexico, according to the State Department, and Mexico City is the fifth rated destination for digital nomads globally, according to nomadlist.com.

While foreigners have reaped the benefits of cheaper housing as they spend money on the local economy, some critics say it's created more inequality for local Mexicans who are feeling priced out.

The influx of expats with high purchasing power has led to viral videos of local residents condemning them for higher living costs and gentrification in the capital city.

Martin Naranjo, a Mexico City resident, drew attention to this issue in a TikTok video, decrying that locally owned taco stands and bodegas are turning into yoga studios and cafes in certain areas. He spoke about people having to go further away from the city to find affordable rent, food and entertainment as prices climbed in recent years.

13. The key point of the passage is

(A) to encourage people to move to Mexico

(B) to discourage people to move to Mexico

(C) to convince people to start a business in Mexico

(D) to educate readers of the effects of migrants to the locals of Mexico

14. What was Derrick Morgan's reason in moving to Mexico?

(A) warm weather, relaxed Covid restrictions and cheaper living expenses

(B) job opportunities   (C) business opportunities   (D) he married a local

15. How were the locals of Mexico affected by the influx of people migrating?

(A) people having to go further away from the city to find affordable rent, food and entertainment as prices climbed

(B) business opportunities rose for the locals as more expats migrate

(C) locals are getting more modernized as they get influenced by the migrants

(D) living expenses become cheaper

16. What is a "snowbird" according to the passage?

(A) someone who enjoys the snow

(B) someone who stays in short-term rental properties during fall and winter

(C) a local resident   (D) someone who permanently moved to a place

17. In line 12, what does the underlined word mean?

(A) boring   (B) tedious   (C) alluring   (D) offensive

18. In line 20, what does the underlined word mean?

(A) decrease   (B) decline   (C) absence   (D) flood

Questions 19–24

Many Americans turn to the latest big idea to lose weight—fad diets, fitness crazes, dodgy herbs and pills, bariatric surgery, just to name a few. They're rarely the magic solution people dream of.

Now a wave of startups offer access to a new category of drugs coupled with intensive behavioral coaching online. But already concerns are emerging.

These startups, spurred by hundreds of millions of dollars in funding from blue-chip venture capital firms, have signed up well over 100,000 patients and could reach millions more. These patients pay hundreds, if not thousands, of dollars, to access new drugs, called GLP-1 agonists, along with online coaching to encourage healthy habits.

The startups initially positioned themselves in lofty terms. "This is the last weight loss program you'll try," said a 2020 marketing analysis by startup Calibrate Health, in messaging designed to reach one of its target demographics, the "Working Mom." (Company spokesperson

Michelle Wellington said the document does not reflect Calibrate's current marketing strategy.)

But while doctors and patients are intrigued by the new model, some customers complain online that reality is short of the buildup: They say they got canned advice and unresponsive clinicians—and some report they couldn't get the newest drugs.

Dr. Scott Butsch, director of obesity medicine at the Cleveland Clinic, said the startups can offer care with less judgment and stigma than in-person peers. They're also more convenient.

Butsch, who learned about the model through consultancies, patients, and colleagues, wonders whether the startups are operating "to strategically find which patients respond to which drug." He said they should coordinate well with behavioral specialists, as antidepressants or other medications may be driving weight gain. "Obesity is a complex disease and requires treatments that match its complexity," he said. "I think programs that do not have a multidisciplinary team are less comprehensive and, in the long term, less effective."

19. The key point of the passage is

(A) to educate people the perks and disadvantages of the latest weight loss method from startups that offer new category of drugs coupled with behavioral coaching

(B) to discourage people to try the wave of startups offer access to a new category of drugs coupled with intensive behavioral coaching

(C) to advertise fad diets, fitness crazes, dodgy herbs and pills, bariatric surgery

(D) to prove that fad diets, fitness crazes, dodgy herbs and pills, bariatric surgery are not effective

20. Which among the list below is not considered a weight loss method?

(A) fad diets　(B) colostomy　(C) fitness crazes　(D) dodgy herbs and pills

21. What is the name of the new drug offered by the weight loss startups?

(A) *Camellia sinensis*　(B) GLP-2　(C) GLP-1　(D) GLP-3

22. In line 2, what does the underlined word mean?

(A) standard　(B) classic　(C) proven　(D) trend

23. In line 10, what part of speech is the underlined word?

(A) driven　(B) halted　(C) paused　(D) discouraged

24. What is Dr. Butsch's stand on the startups?

(A) he promotes the startups as 99% effective

(B) he believes that programs that do not have a multidisciplinary team are less comprehensive and, in the long term, less effective

(C) he completely disapproves the startups as they've shown 0% effectiveness

(D) he doesn't have a stand

Questions 25–30

A recent experiment suggests that money can indeed buy happiness—at least for six months, among households making up to $123,000 a year.

A study published Monday in the journal *PNAS* looked at the effects of giving 200 people a one-time sum of $10,000.

The money, which came from two anonymous wealthy donors, was distributed on PayPal through a partnership with the organization TED.

Participants who got the money were required to spend it all within three months. They recorded how happy they felt on a monthly basis, as did a control group of 100 people who did not get any money. The researchers measured happiness by having people rank how satisfied they were with their lives on a scale of 1 to 7 and how frequently they experienced positive feelings, like happiness, and negative feelings, such as sadness, on a scale of 1 to 5.

The group that got $10,000 reported higher levels of happiness than those who did not after their three months of spending. Then, after three more months had passed, the recipients still reported levels of happiness higher than when the experiment started.

However, people with household incomes above $123,000 did not report noticeable improvements in their happiness.

The participants recorded how they spent their money, but the researchers are still analyzing the data to see whether any types of purchases led to the most happiness.

Those in the study came from three low-income countries—Brazil, Indonesia and Kenya—and four high-income countries: Australia, Canada, the United Kingdom and the U.S. The findings indicated that participants from the low-income countries gained three times as much happiness as those from high-income countries. And people who earned $10,000 a year gained twice as much happiness as those making $100,000 annually.

25. The key point of the passage is

(A) to prove that you need money to be happy

(B) to encourage people to stay at the low-income bracket to be happier

(C) to inform readers of a recent experiment suggesting that money can indeed buy happiness under certain conditions

(D) to invite people to earn more money to be happier

26. What population were part of the study?

(A) three low-income countries—Brazil, Indonesia and Kenya

(B) four high-income countries: Australia, Canada, the United Kingdom and the U.S.

(C) 200 random people from the U.S.

(D) both B and C

27. Higher income household are happier than those who received the $10,000 from the study. True or False?

(A) true   (B) false

28. How was happiness measured from the study?

(A) having people rank how satisfied they were with their lives on a scale of 1 to 7

(B) how frequently they experienced positive feelings, like happiness, on a scale of 1 to 5

(C) how frequently they experienced negative feelings, such as sadness, on a scale of 1 to 5

(D) all of the above

29. How many months were the participants required to spend the money from the study?

(A) 1 month   (B) 6 months   (C) 3 months   (D) 1 year

30. How many participants were given $10,000 to study effect of money on happiness?

(A) 200   (B) 3   (C) 7   (D) 100

Questions 31–36

Since the beginning of the pandemic, the mercurial nature of the coronavirus has been on display. Some people get mild, cold-like illnesses or even have no symptoms when infected, while other people become severely ill and may die from COVID-19.

What determines that fate is complicated and somewhat mysterious. Researchers are looking at a wide variety of factors that may play a role —everything from demographics to preexisting conditions to vaccination status and even genetic clues.

But young and otherwise healthy people may get really sick, be hospitalized or even die from COVID-19 too. It's hard to predict who might succumb, but researchers are searching for genetic clues.

Some studies have found that versions of genes inherited from Neanderthals may protect against COVID-19, while other genetic heirlooms passed down from Neanderthals can up the risk of severe disease (SN: 2/17/21; SN: 10/2/20).

A massive international study examining DNA from more than 28,000 COVID-19 patients and almost 600,000 people who hadn't been infected (to the best of their knowledge) confirmed that inheritance from Neandertals is involved in COVID-19 susceptibility.

The study also confirmed a previous finding that people with type O blood may have some protection against getting infected with the coronavirus (SN: 7/8/21). Exactly what accounts for the protection is still not known.

People with rare variants in a gene called toll-like receptor 7, or TLR7, are 5.3 times more likely to get severe COVID-19 than those who don't have the variants, the team also reported November 3 in PLOS Genetics. Biologically, the link makes sense. TLR7's protein is involved in signaling the immune system that a virus has invaded. Part of its duties include marshaling interferons, immune system chemicals that are some of the first responders to viral infections (SN: 8/6/20). Interferons warn cells to raise their antiviral defenses and help to kill infected cells.

31. The key point of the passage is

(A) to educate people of the role genes play in susceptibility to COVID-19

(B) to encourage people to only mate with those whose genes offer protection to the virus

(C) to advertise DNA testing and get tested

(D) to convince people that susceptibility to the virus is just random

32. The reason why people with type O blood may have some protection against getting infected with the coronavirus is still unknown. True or false?

(A) false   (B) true

33. What gene will make someone be 5.3 times more likely to get severe COVID-19?

(A) PLOS Genetics   (B) Type 0   (C) TLR7   (D) Neanderthals

34. Why do people with this rare genetic variant more prone to get severe COVID-19 than those who don't?

(A) it is still unknown

(B) this genetic variant attracts the virus more

(C) TLR7 makes the body conducive breeding ground of the virus as it does not signal the cells when a virus invades the body

(D) TLR7's protein is involved in signaling the immune system that a virus has invaded which warn cells to raise their antiviral defenses and help to kill infected cells

35. What factors are researchers looking into to pinpoint how someone is more susceptible to coronavirus and get severe symptoms?

(A) demographics   (B) preexisting conditions and vaccination status

(C) genetic clues   (D) all of the above

36. In line 2, what does the underlined word mean?

(A) stable   (B) erratic   (C) constant   (D) steady

End of section.

If you have any time left, go over the questions in this section only.

Do not start the next section.

You have 40 minutes to answer the 47 questions in the Mathematics Achievement Section.

Each question is followed by four suggested answers. Read each question and then decide which one of the four suggested answers is best.

Find the row of spaces on your document that has the same number as the question. In this row, mark the space having the same letter as the answer you have chosen. You may write in your test booklet.

SAMPLE QUESTION:

Which of the numbers below is not factor of 364?

(A) 13
(B) 20
(C) 26
(D) 91

The correct answer is 20, so circle B is darkened.

Sample Answer

A ● C D

---

1. By selling of 25 books, a bookseller gained the selling price of five books as profit. His gain percent is:

   (A) 20% (B) 25% (C) 12% (D) 30%

2. Twenty kilograms of wheat costing $42 per kg is mixed with 5 kg of wheat costing $52 per kg. The price of mixed wheat is:

   (A) 48 (B) 45 (C) 44 (D) 42

3. What is the value of 10 r 8 s 4 t 2 u 5, when r = +, s = ÷, t = ×, u = –

   (A) –8 (B) 10 (C) 21 (D) 9

4. $1,620.08 - 164 \div 8 + 61 = ?$

   (A) 1,660.58 (B) 1,074.55 (C) 1,947.52 (D) 1,660

5. $180 \div 9.5 = ?$

   (A) 20 (B) 18.95 (C) 10.24 (D) 34.25

6. Find the suitable alternative to complete the series?

   −6, −4, −2, 0, _____?

   (A) 0   (B) 2   (C) 5   (D) 8

7. The G.C.M. of two numbers is 14 and their sum is 140. The quantity of such number pairings is:

   (A) 2   (B) 3   (C) 4   (D) 5

8. 15,420 + 16,902 ÷ ? = 21,054

   (A) 1   (B) 2   (C) 3   (D) 4

9. The arrangement of the number $\sqrt{10}, \frac{18}{5}$ and $\frac{102}{78}$ in increasing order from left to right is:

   (A) $\frac{102}{78}, \sqrt{10}, \frac{18}{5}$ (B) $\frac{18}{5}, \sqrt{10}, \frac{102}{78}$ (C) $\sqrt{10}, \frac{18}{5}, \frac{102}{78}$ (D) $\frac{102}{78}, \frac{18}{5}, \sqrt{10}$

10. Simplified value of $\dfrac{(100.1)^3 - (0.1)^3}{(100.1)^2 + (10.01) + (0.1)^2}$

    (A) 100   (B) 200   (C) 90.88   (D) 99.01

11. In triangle QRS, find the value of $x°$.

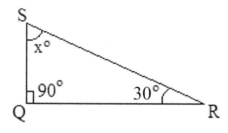

    (A) 60°   (B) 63°   (C) 27°   (D) 50°

12. $p^3 + 3p^2q + 3pq^2 + q^3 = ?$

    (A) $(p - q)^3$ (B) $(p + q)^3$ (C) $p^3 - q^3$ (D) $p^2 + q^2$

13. $3^6 - 3^3 = ?$

    (A) 810   (B) 712   (C) 702   (D) 700

14. Find the missing number

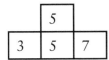

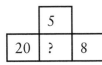

	5	
20	?	8

(A) 7 (B) 11 (C) 9 (D) 1

Questions 15–20

Refer to the following graph.

Study the table carefully and answer the given questions.

Data regarding number of events booked/held at five different halls in 2016.

Halls	Number of Events Booked	Number of Events Cancelled	Out of Events Held, Percentage of Marriage Receptions
A	242	32	80%
B	254	30	75%
C	210	35	80%
D	280	55	80%
E	265	25	85%
Note: Number of events held = Number of events booked – Number of events cancelled.			

15. What was the respective ratio between number of events held at Hall B and those held at Hall E?

(A) 3:5 (B) 5:7 (C) 14:15 (D) 7:9

16. The number of events that were not marriage receptions at Hall A was what percent less than the number of events that were not marriage receptions at Hall E?

(A) $57\frac{1}{7}$ (B) $48\frac{1}{7}$ (C) $14\frac{2}{7}$ (D) $16\frac{2}{3}$

17. At Hall B in 2018, if number of events held was $1\frac{3}{8}$ times that in 2016 and number of events cancelled increased by 30% over that in 2016, how many events were booked?

(A) 282 (B) 278 (C) 324 (D) 347

18. What was the average number of marriage receptions held at Halls A, B, and C?

(A) 158.66　(B) 156.88　(C) 148.22　(D) 172.21

19. What was the difference between total number of events held at Halls B and E together and those cancelled at the same halls together?

(A) 409　(B) 383　(C) 403　(D) 398

20. A starts a certain business with $5,000. Three months from the start of the business, B joins with an amount which is $1,000 more than that invested by A. Nine months from the start of the business, B leaves and C joins, with an amount which is $2,000 more than that invested by B. If B's share from the annual profit is $60,000, what is the annual profit earned?

(A) $120,000　(B) $72,000　(C) $200,000　(D) $54,000

21. In a school 44% of the students play football and 52% students play cricket. If 10% of the students neither play football nor cricket, then what is the percentage of the students playing both?

(A) 40%　(B) 6%　(C) 2%　(D) 22%

22. Find the H.C.F. of 48, 60, and 108.

(A) 12　(B) 5　(C) 18　(D) 17

23. $\dfrac{360 \times 24 \times 4 \times 21}{24 \times 24 \times 20} = ?$

(A) 63　(B) 73　(C) 35　(D) 70

24. 1,025.88 ÷ 4

(A) 256.47　(B) 361.20　(C) 582.54　(D) 12.151

25. $15^2 = ?$

(A) 225　(B) 685　(C) 289　(D) none of the above

26. 45 ÷ 0.25 = ?

(A) 160　(B) 980　(C) 180　(D) 190

27. Find the L.C.M of 12, 24, and 30.

(A) 160　(B) 220　(C) 240　(D) 204

28. If $x = 10$ and $y = 5$, find the value of $3x^2 + 2y$.

(A) 325　(B) 310　(C) 250　(D) 287

29. $900 \div 25 = 360 -$ _____.

(A) 324   (B) 239   (C) 311   (D) 219

30. $\dfrac{3}{5}\% = ?$

(A) $\dfrac{3}{40}$ (B) $\dfrac{3}{500}$ (C) $\dfrac{3}{250}$ (D) $\dfrac{1}{100}$

31. Two trains leave Delhi for Kolkata at 6 a.m. and 6:45 a.m. Their speeds are 100 km/hr and 136 km/hr, respectively. At what distance (in km) from Delhi will the two trains meet?

(A) 267.5   (B) 250   (C) 283.33   (D) 275

32. If $\dfrac{x}{x+2} = \dfrac{4}{5}$, what is the value of x?

(A) 4   (B) 8   (C) 6   (D) 7

33. $8 : 64 :: 9 : ?$

(A) 50   (B) 72   (C) 81   (D) 64

34. If $s = 634.25$ and $t = 32.57$, then find the value of s/t.

(A) 22.15   (B) 20.25   (C) 19.47   (D) 35.65

35. $\dfrac{8.5 \times 0.75}{0.0018 \times 0.19} = ?$

(A) 18,640.3   (B) 11,250.6   (C) 12,555.5   (D) 22,500.9

36. Find the wrong number of the given series

462   422   380   342   306

(A) 420   (B) 422   (C) 306   (D) none of the above

37. The product of two numbers is 4,107. If the H.C.F. of the numbers is 37, the greater number is:

(A) 55   (B) 75   (C) 111   (D) 121

38. If $\cos^2\theta + \cos\theta = 1$, then find the value of $(\sin^4\theta + \sin^2\theta)$.

(A) 1   (B) 2   (C) 0   (D) $\sqrt{2}$

39. What sum of money will become $1,360 in two years at 3% p.a. compound interest?

(A) $1,200.8   (B) $1,225.6   (C) $1,281.9   (D) $1,300.7

40. Ten percent discount and then 30% discount in succession is equivalent to total discount of:

    (A) 15% (B) 28% (C) 31% (D) 37%

41. What is the least common multiple of 8, 13, and 21?

    (A) 1,063 (B) 2,184 (C) 1,224 (D) 1,226

42. $\dfrac{5}{6} \times \dfrac{36}{45} =$

    (A) $\dfrac{2}{3}$ (B) $\dfrac{8}{7}$ (C) $\dfrac{3}{2}$ (D) $\dfrac{7}{2}$

43. The perimeter of one face of a cube is 36 cm. Its volume will be:

    (A) 252 cm³ (B) 729 cm³ (C) 400 cm³ (D) 625 cm³

44. Which of the following is equivalent to $\dfrac{6}{16}x = 14 + 3y$?

    (A) $6x - 48y = 224$ (B) $15x - 13y = 163$ (C) $15x - 13y = 144$ (D) $25x - 26y = 156$

45. If $\dfrac{a}{b} + \dfrac{b}{a} = 4$, then what is the value of $a^2 + b^2$?

    (A) $2ab$ (B) $4ab$ (C) $8ab$ (D) $6ab$

46. Allowing 10% and 20% successive discounts, the selling price of an article becomes $720, then the market price will be:

    (A) $1,000 (B) $3,000 (C) $4,500 (D) $6,000

47. Which of the following is divisible by 37?

    (A) $45 \times 6 - (40 \div 4) + 11\,(3 + 7)$ (B) $45 \times 3 - (20 \div 4) + 4\,(2 + 7)$
    (C) $60 \times 2 - (4 \times 3) + 14\,(3 + 2)$ (D) $46 \times 10 \div (5 + 5) + 25\,(1 \times 3)$

End of section.

If you have any time left, go over the questions in this section only.

Do not start the next section.

Essay Topic Sheet

The directions for the Essay portion of the ISEE are printed in the box below. Use the pre-lined pages on pages 167 and 168 for this part of the Practice Test.

You will have 30 minutes to plan and write an essay on the topic printed on the other side of this page. **Do not write on another topic. An essay on another topic is not acceptable.**

The essay is designed to give you an opportunity to show how well you can write. You should try to express your thoughts clearly. How well you write is much more important than how much you write, but you need to say enough for a reader to understand what you mean.

You will probably want to write more than a short paragraph. You should also be aware that a copy of your essay will be sent to each school that will be receiving your test results. You are to write only in the appropriate section of the answer sheet. Please write or print so that your writing may be read by someone who is not familiar with your handwriting.

You may make notes and plan your essay on the reverse side of the page. Allow enough time to copy the final form onto your answer sheet. You must copy the essay topic onto your answer sheet, in the box provided.

Please remember to write only the final draft of the essay on your answer sheet and to write it in blue or black pen. Again, you may use cursive writing or you may print. Only pages 171 and 172 will be sent to the schools.

Directions continue on the next page.

REMINDER: Please write this essay topic on the first few lines of your answer sheet.

Essay Topic

What is your most memorable event this year and why?

- Only write on this essay question
- Only pages 167 and 168 will be sent to the schools
- Only write in blue or black pen

NOTES

_____

_____

_____

_____

_____

_____

_____

_____

_____

_____

_____

_____

_____

_____

_____

_____

_____

STUDENT NAME _____ GRADE APPLYING FOR _____

Use a blue or black ballpoint pen to write the final draft of your essay on this sheet.

You must write your essay topic in this space.

_____

_____

_____

Use specific details in your response

_____

_____

_____

_____

_____

_____

_____

_____

_____

_____

_____

_____

_____

_____

_____

_____

_____

_____

_____

End of section.

If you have any time left, go over the questions in this section only.

ANSWER KEY

Verbal Reasoning

1. A	9. A	17. B	25. C	33. A
2. C	10. C	18. B	26. B	34. A
3. B	11. B	19. A	27. A	35. D
4. B	12. D	20. C	28. C	36. B
5. D	13. B	21. A	29. C	37. A
6. D	14. C	22. D	30. B	38. A
7. B	15. A	23. D	31. B	39. B
8. A	16. D	24. B	32. D	40. C

1. The correct answer is (A). Flair refers to a skill or instinctive ability to appreciate or make good use of something, talent. It can also refer to a uniquely attractive quality or style.

2. The correct answer is (C). To ferret means to search tenaciously for and find something. Synonyms are to explore, uncover, and discover.

3. The correct answer is (B). Gingerly is an adjective which means showing great care or caution. It can also be used as an adverb which means in a careful or cautious manner.

    Sample (adjective): "His questions were gingerly and puzzled."—John Skow

    Sample (adverb): "Jackson sat down very gingerly"

4. The correct answer is (B). Glut means an excessively abundant supply of something.

5. The correct answer is (D). To grapple means to struggle with or work hard to deal with or overcome (a difficulty or challenge).

6. The correct answer is (D). To inaugurate means to begin or introduce (a system, policy, or period).

7. The correct answer is (B). To vie means to compete eagerly with someone to do or achieve something.

8. The correct answer is (A). Voracious means wanting or devouring great quantities of food. It can also mean having a very eager approach to an activity. Synonyms are greedy, keen, and avid.

9. The correct answer is (A). A cynic is a person who distrusts other people and believes that everything is done for selfish reasons. It refers to a person who questions whether something will happen or whether it is worthwhile. Synonyms are skeptic, pessimist, and quitter.

10. The correct answer is (C). Debilitating means causing serious impairment of strength or ability to function. Synonyms are enervating, exhausting, and disheartening.

11. The correct answer is (B). Dearth means a scarcity or lack of something.

12. The correct answer is (D). To feign means to pretend to be affected by (a feeling, state, or injury). Synonyms are to fake, act, and sham.

13. The correct answer is (B). Gist refers to the substance or essence of a speech or text.

14. The correct answer is (C). A connoisseur is an expert judge in matters of taste.

15. The correct answer is (A). Loath means reluctant; unwilling. To loathe means to feel intense dislike or disgust for.

16. The correct answer is (D). To abase means to behave in a way that belittles or degrades (someone). Synonyms are to degrade, demean, and disgrace.

17. The correct answer is (B). To abscond means to leave hurriedly and secretly, typically to avoid detection of or arrest for an unlawful action such as theft.

18. The correct answer is (B). To abate means to (of something perceived as hostile, threatening, or negative) become less intense or widespread. Synonyms are to subside, faded, and decrease.

19. The correct answer is (A). To accede means to give or express one's approval (as to a proposal). Synonyms are to agree, accept, and consent.

20. The correct answer is (C). Abject means (of something bad) experienced or present to the maximum degree. It also means (of a person or their behavior) completely without pride or dignity, self-abasing. Synonyms are humble, meek, and menial.

21. The correct answer is (A). "A blessing in disguise" is a commonly used phrase which means a good thing that seemed bad at first. In this sentence, it was a good thing it rained because the test got cancelled. Disguise means a cover-up, facade, or a mask.

22. The correct answer is (D). "Cutting someone some slack" is a commonly used phrase which means to not judge someone as severely. Slack means not taut or held tightly in position; loose.

23. The correct answer is (D). To abridge means to make less in extent or duration. In this sentence, her curfew is shortened after getting the highest scores.

24. The correct answer is (B). To accost means to approach and address (someone) boldly or aggressively. In this sentence, she stays at home after being approached aggressively by reporters. The sentence may be referring to a celebrity or a public figure.

25. The correct answer is (C). Aghast means filled with horror or shock. Synonyms are horrified, appalled, and shocked.

26. The correct answer is (B). To allay means to make more bearable or less severe.

27. The correct answer is (A). An amble means a relaxed journey on foot for exercise or pleasure. Synonyms are stroll, walk, and wander.

28. The correct answer is (C). Baleful means threatening harm; menacing. In this sentence, Billy looked at his bullies with his threatening eyes as he finally fought back.

29. The correct answer is (C). Belligerent means hostile and aggressive. In this sentence, the waitress reported an aggressive guest who started a fight with the next table.

30. The correct answer is (B). To bilk means to obtain (money) fraudulently. In this sentence, the neighbor got money from passing fake solicitations to clueless elderly, so he was arrested.

31. The correct answer is (B). Cogent means having the power to persuade. Synonyms are compelling, convincing, and conclusive.

32. The correct answer is (D). Collusion means a secret or illegal cooperation or conspiracy, especially to cheat or deceive others. In this sentence, Sergeant Claire didn't know what the armed forces and the drug traffickers are plotting.

33. The correct answer is (A). Deft means demonstrating skill and cleverness. In this sentence, Alice won numerous awards due to her skill in arts.

34. The correct answer is (A). Derelict means in a very poor condition because of disuse and neglect.

35. The correct answer is (D). Despondent means in low spirits from loss of hope or courage.

36. The correct answer is (B). To extol means to praise enthusiastically.

37. The correct answer is (A). A fabulist is a liar, especially a person who invents elaborate, dishonest stories.

38. The correct answer is (A). To exult means to feel or express joy or triumph. In the sentence, after facing several crises on their project, the team rewarded themselves with a vacation for their success.

39. The correct answer is (B). To abet means to provide (someone) with what is useful or necessary to achieve an end. In this sentence, the villain will facilitate the main character's failure so he can look bad on the king's eyes.

40. The correct answer is (C). Atrocious means extremely disturbing or repellent. In this sentence, because the crime was so horrific, nobody likes to remember or talk about it.

Quantitative Reasoning

1. A	11. D	21. B	31. C
2. D	12. C	22. D	32. B
3. C	13. B	23. A	33. C
4. A	14. A	24. A	34. B
5. D	15. B	25. B	35. A
6. A	16. B	26. A	36. A
7. A	17. A	27. B	37. C
8. C	18. A	28. A	
9. B	19. C	29. B	
10. A	20. B	30. D	

1. The correct answer is (A).

    According to question

    $20 \times 4 \div 3 - 2 + 1 \Longrightarrow 20 \div 4 + 3 \times 2 - 1 = 10$

2. The correct answer is (D).

3. The correct answer is (C). $9,24,580 = 9,00,000 + 20,000 + 4,000 + 500 + 80 + 0$
    So, the answer is 20,000.

4. The correct answer is (A). $3^2 + 4^2 = 9 + 16 = 25 = 5^2$

5. The correct answer is (D). $(P) \Longrightarrow 3^5 = 243$, $(Q) \Longrightarrow 5^3 = 125$, $(R) \Longrightarrow 3^5 \times 5^3 = 30,375$

6. The correct answer is (A). The circumference of the circle $= \pi d$ unit where d is the diameter, therefore circumference $= 10\,\pi$ cm

7. The correct answer is (A). $103 \times 97 = (100 + 3)(100 - 3) = 100^2 - 3^2 = 9,991$

8. Answer: Option C

    There are two alphabetical series here. The first series is with the first letters only: STUVW. The second series involves the remaining letters: CD, EF, GH, IJ, KL.

9. Answer: Option B

    Because the letters are the same, concentrate on the number series, which is a simple 2, 3, 4, 5, 6 series, and follows each letter in order.

10. Answer: Option A

    The middle letters are static, so concentrate on the first and third letters. The series involves an alphabetical order with a reversal of the letters. The first letters are in alphabetical order: F, G, H, I, J. The second and fourth segments are reversals of the first and third segments. The missing segment begins with a new letter.

11. Answer: Option D

    The second and fourth letters in the series, L and A, are static. The first and third letters consist of an alphabetical order beginning with the letter E.

12. Answer: Option C

    The first letters are in alphabetical order with a letter skipped in between each segment: C, E, G, I, K. The second and third letters are repeated; they are also in order with a skipped letter: M, O, Q, S, U.

13. The correct answer is (B). Starting with the top left figure, one line is increasing in each figure while moving in the clockwise direction. So, four lines will come four parts.

14. The correct answer is (A).

    According to the question, total number of candidates = 500

    Candidates failed in Math and History = 12

    Candidates failed in Math and English = 12

    Candidates failed in English and History = 10

    Candidates failed in three subjects = 5

    So, the number of candidates who failed in at least three subjects = 5

    $\therefore$ Percentage $= \dfrac{5}{500} \times 100 = 1\%$

15. The correct answer is (B). $(8 \times 15 \div 5) - 16 \times 3 \div 8 = 24 - 6 = 18$.

16. The correct answer is (B).

    $4x + 2 = 22$

    $\implies x = 20 \div 4$

    $\implies x = 5$.

    $\therefore 20x + 50 = 20 \times 5 + 50 = 150$.

17. The correct answer is (A). $\dfrac{x^2}{5} + 12 = \dfrac{4}{5} + 12 = 64 / 5$.

18. The correct answer is (A). Half of the perimeter $= 2a = 2 \times 30 = 60$ ft.

19. The correct answer is (C). $\sqrt[4]{625} = \sqrt[4]{5 \times 5 \times 5 \times 5} = 5$.

20. The correct answer is (B). $\dfrac{64}{7} \div \dfrac{8}{49} = \dfrac{64}{7} \times \dfrac{49}{8} = 8 \times 7 = 56$.

21. The correct answer is (B). Here $x = 180° - 60° = 120°$, therefore two quantities are equal. Here $x = 180° - 70° = 110°$, therefore Column B is greater than Column A.

22. The correct answer is (D). The relationship cannot be determined from this information because we cannot find x and y individually with this information, we only have $xy = 56$.

23. The correct answer is (A). Here $\sqrt{64} + \sqrt{25} = 13$ and $\sqrt{25 + 64} = 9.43$.

24. The correct answer is (A). Here the area is 16, one side of the quadrilateral is 4, then the other side will be 4. Now the perimeter will be $= 2 \times (4 + 4) = 16$ unit. So, Column A is greater.

25. The correct answer is (B). john had $20. He gave half of her money to his sister so now he has $= 10. Also, Jenny has now $30. So, Column B is greater.

26. The correct answer is (A). Here $2x + 3 = 13$, then $2x = 10$, so $x = 5$, and $\dfrac{y}{2} = 2$, then $y = 4$.

27. The correct answer is (B). The area of the rectangle $= 10 \times 5 = 50$ sq. unit and the area of the square $= 8 \times 8$ sq. unit $= 64$ sq. unit. Therefore, Column B is greater.

28. The correct answer is (A). The average number of chocolates $= 4$, and the number of chocolates eaten on Friday is 3. So, Column A is greater.

29. The correct answer is (B). Here $100 > 1.00$ therefore $\sqrt{100} > \sqrt{1.00}$.

30. The correct answer is (D). The relationship cannot be determined from the information which is given in this question. Here we don't know the price for one orange and one peach.

31. The correct answer is (C). Here $-(2)^5 = -32$ and $(-2)^5 = -32$, both are equal.

32. The correct answer is (B). $A = 11$, $B = 12$, hence $B > A$.

33. The correct answer is (C). The prime numbers are 1, 3, 5 and the even numbers are 2, 4, 6. So the probability of even number and the probability of prime numbers are both ½ hence equal.

34. The correct answer is (B). The fractional part of the figure that is shaded $= \dfrac{3}{20}$. So, B is greater.

35. The correct answer is (A). 50% of 20 slices = 10 and one-fourth of the pizza = 0.25 × 20 = 5. Therefore, Column A is greater.

36. The correct answer is (A). $100 – $20 = $80 – $16 = $64, $100 – 40% disc = $100 – $40 = $60. Hence Column A is greater.

37. The correct answer is (C). The slope $= \dfrac{10-2}{8-4} = 2$ and $3x – y = -8$, then $y = 2x + 18$, therefore the slope = 2. So, both are equal.

Reading Comprehension and Vocabulary

1. A	7. B	13. D	19. A	25. C	31. A
2. B	8. C	14. A	20. B	26. D	32. B
3. C	9. D	15. A	21. C	27. B	33. C
4. D	10. A	16. B	22. D	28. D	34. D
5. A	11. B	17. C	23. A	29. C	35. D
6. A	12. C	18. D	24. B	30. A	36. B

1. The correct answer is (A). The passage is discussing how there is a shortage of pediatric beds which made the Chavezes wait monthlong for a bed to open at their local children's hospital so baby MJ could have the procedure she needed.

2. The correct answer is (B). See lines 1–3.

3. The correct answer is (C). See lines 21–24.

4. The correct answer is (D). See lines 25–30.

5. The correct answer is (A). Agonizing means causing great physical or mental pain. Synonyms are unbearable, harsh, and cruel.

6. The correct answer is (A). "At a premium" means scarce and in demand. Synonyms are rare and tin on the ground.

7. The correct answer is (B). The example of the passage may be Christine Applegate, but the passage focuses on how one can overlook the symptoms of multiple sclerosis which was the case of the actress.

8. The correct answer is (C). See lines 2–3.

9. The correct answer is (D). See lines 30–31, 39–43.

10. The correct answer is (A). See lines 20–23, 24–27.

11. The correct answer is (B). To overlook means to fail to notice (something).

12. The correct answer is (C). To attribute means to regard something as being caused by (someone or something). Synonyms are to scribe, credit, and blame.

13. The correct answer is (D). The passage talked about how the influx of expats increased living costs for the locals which displaced locals by having to go further away from the city to find affordable rent, food, and entertainment.

14. The correct answer is (A). See lines 6–14.

15. The correct answer is (A). See lines 41–44.

16. The correct answer is (B). See lines 9–11.

17. The correct answer is (C). Enticing means attractive or tempting, alluring.

18. The correct answer is (D). Influx means an arrival or entry of large numbers of people or things.

19. The correct answer is (A). The passage talked about experiences of users of the startups that offer intensive behavioral coaching online in combination with a new category of drugs. It was discussed that this new platform is more convenient as it can be done thru an app and can offer care with less judgment and stigma than in-person peers. Many, though, said that when they encounter issues, the responses could have been quicker. This gives an idea to readers to weigh in its perks and downsides.

20. The correct answer is (B). See lines 2–3.

21. The correct answer is (C). See line 15.

22. The correct answer is (D). A fad means an intense and widely shared enthusiasm for something, especially one that is short-lived and without basis in the object's qualities, a craze.

23. The correct answer is (A). To spur means to promote the development of; stimulate. Synonyms are to urge, drive, and encourage.

24. The correct answer is (B). See lines 44–47.

25. The correct answer is (C). The passage was about a study conducted to prove that money can indeed buy happiness at least for six months, among households making up to $123,000 a year. See lines 1–4.

26. The correct answer is (D). See lines 34–37.

27. The correct answer is (B). See lines 21–29, lines 40–43.

28. The correct answer is (D). See lines 15–20.

29. The correct answer is (C). See lines 11–12.

30. The correct answer is (A). See line 6.

31. The correct answer is (A). The passage was discussing how genetic factors such genes inherited from the Neanderthals, blood type and having a rare genetic variant play a role in COVID-19 susceptibility.

32. The correct answer is (B). See lines 32–33.

33. The correct answer is (C). See lines 34–37.

34. The correct answer is (D). See lines 38–45.

35. The correct answer is (D). See lines 10–12.

36. The correct answer is (B). Mercurial means subject to sudden or unpredictable changes of mood or mind. Synonyms are volatile, erratic, and unpredictable.

Mathematics Achievement

1. B	11. A	21. B	31. C	41. B
2. C	12. B	22. A	32. B	42. A
3. D	13. C	23. A	33. B	43. B
4. A	14. B	24. A	34. C	44. A
5. B	15. C	25. A	35. A	45. B
6. B	16. D	26. C	36. B	46. A
7. D	17. D	27. C	37. C	47. A
8. C	18. A	28. B	38. A	
9. A	19. A	29. A	39. C	
10. A	20. C	30. B	40. D	

1. The correct answer is (B).

    Let, selling price of 25 books is $25

    So, selling price of 5 books is $5

    ∴ Purchasing price = 25 – 5 = $20

    ∴ Profit = $5

    ∴ Percentage of Profit = $\left(\dfrac{5 \times 100}{20}\right)\% = 25\%$

2. The correct answer is (C).

    $(20 \times 42 + 5 \times 52) = 1{,}100$

    Average per kg price = $\dfrac{1{,}100}{25} = 44$.

3. The correct answer is (D).

    $r = +, s = \div, t = \times, u = -$

    $10 \text{ r } 8 \text{ s } 4 \text{ t } 2 \text{ u } 5 = 10 + 8 \div 4 \times 2 - 5 = 10 + 2 \times 2 - 5 = 10 + 4 - 5 = 9$

4. $1{,}620.08 - 164 \div 8 + 61 = 1{,}660.58$. The correct answer is (A).

5. $180 \div 9.5 = 18.94736 = 18.95$. The correct answer is (B).

6. The correct answer is (B).

7. The correct answer is (D).

    $140 \div 14 = 10 \implies 1 + 9 \implies 2 + 8 \implies 3 + 7 \implies 4 + 6 \implies 5 + 5$

    $\therefore$ There are five pairs.

8. The correct answer is (C).

    $15,420 + 16,902 \div x = 21,054$

    $\implies \dfrac{16,902}{x} = 21,054 \quad 15,420$

    $\implies \dfrac{16,902}{x} = 5,634$

    $\implies x = 16,902 \div 5,634 = 3$

9. The correct answer is (A).

    $\sqrt{10} = 3.16\ldots$

    $\dfrac{18}{5} = 3.6$

    $\dfrac{102}{78} = 1.307\ldots$

    $\therefore \dfrac{102}{78}, \sqrt{10}, \dfrac{18}{5}$

10. The correct answer is (A).

    Let, $100.1 = a$ and $0.1 = b$

    $\therefore \dfrac{(a)^3 - (b)^3}{(a)^2 + (ab) + (b)^2} = \dfrac{(a-b)(a^2 + ab + b^2)}{(a^2 + ab + b^2)} = a - b = 100.1 - 0.10 = 100$

11. The correct answer is (A).

    We know the total value of all angles of a triangle is 180°.

    So, 180° – (90° + 30°) = 60°.

12. The correct answer is (B).

    As, $(a + b)^3 = a^3 + 3a^2b + 3ab^2 + b^3,$

    So, $(p + q)^3 = p^3 + 3p^2q + 3pq^2 + q^3$

13. The correct answer is (C).

$3^8 - 3^5 = 6,561 - 243 = 3,618.$

$3^6 - 3^3 = 729 - 27 = 702.$

14. The correct answer is (B).

$\dfrac{11+4+15}{3} = 10,$

$\dfrac{3+5+7}{3} = 5,$

$\therefore ? = \dfrac{20+5+8}{3} = 11.$

15. The correct answer is (C).

Number of events in Hall C $\Longrightarrow 210 - 35 = 175$

Number of events in Hall D $\Longrightarrow 280 - 55 = 225$

$\therefore$ Required ratio $= 175:225 = 7:9$

16. The correct answer is (D).

Number of events held in Hall E $\Longrightarrow 265 - 25 = 240$

$\therefore$ Non-marriage reception events $\Longrightarrow \dfrac{240 \times 15}{100} = 36$

Number of events held in Hall A $\Longrightarrow 242 - 32 = 210$

$\therefore$ Non-marriage reception events $\Longrightarrow \dfrac{210 \times 20}{100} = 42$

$\Longrightarrow$ Required percent

$\Longrightarrow \left(\dfrac{42-36}{36}\right) \times 100 = 16\dfrac{2}{3}$

17. The correct answer is (D).

Number of events held in Hall B in 2016 $\Longrightarrow 254 - 30 = 224$

$\therefore$ Number of events held in 2018 $= 224 \times \dfrac{11}{8} = 308$

Number of events cancelled in 2018 $= \dfrac{30 \times 130}{100} = 39$

$\therefore$ Number of events booked $= 308 + 39 = 347$

18. The correct answer is (A).

Number of marriage receptions held:

Hall A $\Longrightarrow \dfrac{210 \times 80}{100} = 168$

Hall B $\Longrightarrow \dfrac{224 \times 75}{200} = 168$

Hall C $\Longrightarrow \dfrac{175 \times 80}{100} = 140$

∴ Required average $= \dfrac{168 + 168 + 140}{3} = 158.66$ approx.

19. The correct answer is (A).

Required difference = (224 + 240) – (25 + 30) = 409

20. The correct answer is (C).

Ratio of the shares of A, B, and C = Ratio of the equivalent capitals of A, B, and C for one month

= 5,000 × 12 : 6,000 × 6 : 8,000 × 3 = 5 : 3 : 2

The sum of the terms of ratio = 5 + 3 + 2 = 10

If total annual profit, be x.

Then B's share = $\$\dfrac{3x}{10}$

∴ $\dfrac{3x}{10} = 60,000$

$\Longrightarrow x = \dfrac{60,000 \times 10}{3} = \$200,000.$

21. The correct answer is (B).

Percentage of students playing both = (52 + 44 + 10) – 100 = 6%

22. The correct answer is (A). H.C.F. of 48, 60, and 108 is 12.

23. The correct answer is (A). $\dfrac{360 \times 24 \times 4 \times 21}{24 \times 24 \times 20} = 63$

24. The correct answer is (A). 1,025.88 ÷ 4 = 256.47

25. The correct answer is (A).

$15^2 = 15 \times 15 = 225.$

26. The correct answer is (C). 45 ÷ 0.25 = 180.

27. The correct answer is (C). L.C.M of 12, 24, and 30 is 240.

28. The correct answer is (B).

$x = 10$ and $y = 5$

So, $3x^2 + 2y = (3 \times 10^2) + (2 \times 5) = (3 \times 100) + 10 = 300 + 10 = 310$.

29. The correct answer is (A).

$900 \div 25 = 360$

$360 - 36 = 324$

30. The correct answer is (B).

$\dfrac{3}{5}\% = \dfrac{3}{5 \times 100} = \dfrac{3}{500}$.

31. The correct answer is (C).

Difference in departure $= 45$ min $= 45/60$ hr $= \dfrac{3}{4}$ hr

Let the meeting distance $= x$.

Time taken to cover x km at 136 kmph be t hr.

Time taken to cover x km at 100 kmph be 45 min more

$= t + \dfrac{3}{4} = \dfrac{4t + 3}{4}$,

Now, $100 \times \dfrac{4t + 3}{4} = 136t$

$100t + 75 = 136t$

$t = \dfrac{75}{36} = 2.083$ hr

Then distance x km $= 136 \times 2.083 \approx 283.33$ km.

32. The correct answer is (B).

$\dfrac{x}{x + 2} = \dfrac{4}{5} \Rightarrow 5x = 4x + 8 \Rightarrow x = 8$

33. The correct answer is (B).

$8 \times 1 = 8$, $8 \times 8 = 64$

Similarly, $9 \times 1 = 9$, $9 \times 8 = 72$.

34. The correct answer is (C).

$s = 634.25$ and $t = 32.57$

So, $s/t = 634.25/32.57 = 19.47$ (approx.).

35. The correct answer is (A).

$$\frac{8.5 \times 0.75}{0.0018 \times 0.19} = 18,640.3$$

36. The correct answer is (B).

$462 - 42 = 420$

$420 - 40 = 380$

$380 - 38 = 342$

$342 - 36 = 306$

So, the number 422 is wrong in this series.

37. The correct answer is (C).

Let the no. s be $37a$ and $37b$

Then, $37a \times 37b = 4,170$, $ab = 3$

Now, co-primes with product 3 are (1,3)

38. The correct answer is (A).

$\cos^2\theta + \cos\theta = 1$

$\implies \cos\theta = 1 - \cos^2\theta = \sin^2\theta$

$\sin^4\theta + \sin^2\theta = (\sin^2\theta)^2 + \sin^2\theta = \cos^2\theta + \sin^2\theta = 1$.

39. The correct answer is (C).

Let the principle $= x$

$$\therefore 1,360 = x\left(1 + \frac{3}{100}\right)^2$$

$$\text{or, } 1,360 = x\left(\frac{103}{100}\right)^2$$

$$\text{or, } x = \frac{1,360 \times 100 \times 100}{103 \times 103}$$

or, $x = \$1,281.9$

40. The correct answer is (D).

As per rules $\left[x + y + \dfrac{xy}{100} \right]$

$\Rightarrow -10 - 20 + \dfrac{(-10 \times -20)}{100} = -30 + 2 = 28\%$

As per rules $\left[x + y - \dfrac{xy}{100} \right]$

$= 10 + 30 - \dfrac{(10)(30)}{100} = 10 + 30 - 3 = 37\%$

41. The correct answer is (B).

2,184 is divisible by 8,13, and 21.

42. The correct answer is (A).

$\dfrac{5}{6} \times \dfrac{36}{45} = \dfrac{2}{3}$

43. The correct answer is (B).

Perimeter of one face, $4a = 36$ cm

Side of a cube $= a = 9$ cm

$\therefore$ Volume of cube $= a^3 = (9)^3 = 729$ cm^3

44. The correct answer is (A).

$\dfrac{5}{13}x = 12 + 2y$

$\Longrightarrow 5x = 156 + 26y$

$\Longrightarrow 5x - 26y = 156.$

$\dfrac{6}{16}x = 14 + 3y$

$\Longrightarrow 6x = 224 + 48y$

$\Longrightarrow 6x - 48y = 224.$

45. The correct answer is (B).

$a/b + b/a = 4$

$a^2 + b^2/ab = 4$

$a^2 + b^2 = 4ab$

.

46. The correct answer is (A).

S.P. of an article = 10% and 20%

Successive discount × Marked price of an article

or, $3,060 = \dfrac{90}{100} \times \dfrac{80}{100} \times$ Marked Price

Marked price of an article $= \dfrac{720 \times 100 \times 100}{80 \times 90} = \$1,000$.

47. The correct answer is (A).

$45 \times 6 - (40 \div 4) + 11 (3 + 7)$

$= 270 - 10 + 11 \times 10 = 260 + 110 = 370.$ ∴ 370 is divisible by 37.

Sample Essay Response

Many would have answered the pandemic was the most memorable event of their year. How many times have you experienced, and will you experience a pandemic in your lifetime? The entire world was put in a halt. Our routines have been replaced with the new normal. Who would have thought distance and online learning is possible? Who would have thought how important having a health insurance is? Who would have thought that many will see how the healthcare system is not perfect, how overworked our medical staffs are and how life is so fleeting? The pandemic lasted for years and up to this point, some people may still be haunted by it.

The pandemic indeed is my most memorable event for the past years. It may have started in 2019 but I'm still going through its aftermath. It is the most memorable event for me because it paved the way for many realizations I could ever have. The first thing it made me realize is how easy it is to die when you do not have the means to access healthcare. I'm glad my employer provided health insurance and I was able to add my dependents. However, even though, you have the means to afford healthcare, you will face another problem. Every hospital was full, resources were limited, and every staff was overworked. Regardless of the money you have on hand, it cannot guarantee a hospital bed, medicines, and staff to care for you. Many people lost millions to try to survive and many died.

Secondly, the pandemic forced everybody to stay at home which made it possible for families to reconnect. Children, unknowing of the chaos outside their homes, were just happy to be spending more time with their father who leaves the house at the crack of dawn before. My family is composed of working adults and a college student. Because of this, we rarely sit together at the dinner table due to work, studies, and time differences. The pandemic made us enjoy dinner together again which we often get to do only on holidays. Thirdly, I was amazed by the money I unintentionally saved for not going out. At least for me, staying at home and minimizing the time we spend outside for groceries by buying in bulk, made me save more money than when I was intentionally doing it before the pandemic hit. Fourthly, I loved working remotely. I already know that I am an introvert and working at home had not crossed my mind before. I already accepted that I had to be outside in the society to perform my responsibilities. I was more productively as I only focused on meaningful interactions while working at home and even had free time to start a new hobby and do self-care. As for me, the changes the pandemic brought were mostly good.

Finally, I had a lot of time to reflect on life and on what I want to do and happen with my life, professionally and personally. I was never materialistic, but the pandemic just made me realize even more that there are more important things in life than those two-story house and luxury cars. A peaceful life is what I am yearning for and will strive to achieve with the love of my life. Someday, we'll be happy and married. We'll be starting the day slow and enjoying the sunset together far from the worries of life and just enjoying every single moment. I hope that someday will be soon.

For the ISEE, the most commonly referenced score is the stanine score. Check out the four steps to calculating stanine scores.

Step 1: The Raw Score

The first step in scoring is calculating a raw score. This is quite simple.

Students receive one point for each correct answer and no points for incorrect answers or unanswered questions.

Tip: Because there is no score penalty for incorrect answers or unanswered questions, be sure to answer every single question! Answering all of the questions can only increase your chances of a higher score.

Step 2: The Scaled Score

Once a raw score has been calculated for each section, it is converted into a scaled score.

This conversion adjusts for the variation in difficulty between different tests. Thus, a lower raw score on a harder test could give you the same scaled score as a higher raw score on an easier test. This process is called equating.

The scaled score for each section ranges from 760 to 940.

Step 3: The Percentile Score

Next, the percentile score for each section is calculated.

Percentiles compare a student's scaled score to all other same-grade students from the past three years. This is important to understand because the ISEE is taken by students in a range of grades. The Upper Level ISEE, for instance, is taken by students applying to grades 9–12; however, the percentile score is based only on the performance of other students applying to the same grade. Thus, a student applying to 9th grade will not be compared to a student applying to 12th grade.

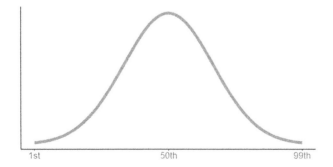

Here's an example to help understand percentile scores: scoring in the 40th percentile indicates that a student scored the same or higher than 40% of students in the same grade but lower than 59% of students.

Step 4: The Stanine Score

Finally, the percentile is converted into a stanine score.

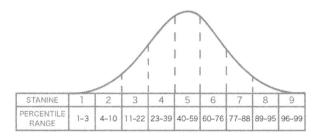

STANINE	1	2	3	4	5	6	7	8	9
PERCENTILE RANGE	1–3	4–10	11–22	23–39	40–59	60–76	77–88	89–95	96–99

Notice that the percentile ranges for the middle stanines of 4–6 are far larger than the ranges for the extreme stanines of 1, 2, 8, or 9. This means that most students taking the ISEE achieve scores in the middle ranges. Only the top 4% of all test takers receive a stanine of 9 on any given section, while 20% of students receive a stanine of 5.

So, what is a good ISEE score?

Stanine scores (which range from 1 to 9) are the most important and are the scores schools pay the most attention to. But what is a good score on the ISEE? A score of 5 or higher will be enough to put students in the running for most schools, although some elite private schools want applicants to have ISEE test results of 7 or higher.

Here's a sample ISEE Report

ISEE® INDEPENDENT SCHOOL
ENTRANCE EXAM

Individual Student Report

Candidate for Grade	8
ID Number	
Gender	**Male**
Date of Birth	**4/8/2004**
Phone Number	
Test Level/Form	**Middle/0916**
Date of Testing	**11/30/2016**
Tracking Number	**201612010592103**

The Test Profile below shows your total scores for each test. Refer to the enclosed brochure called *Understanding the Individual Student Report* to help you interpret the *Test Profile* and *Analysis*. Percentile Ranks and Stanines are derived from norms for applicants to independent schools.

TEST PROFILE

Section	Scaled Score (760 – 940)	Percentile Rank (1 – 99)	Stanine (1 – 9)	Stanine Analysis 1 2 3 4 5 6 7 8 9
Verbal Reasoning	895	90	8	V
Reading Comprehension	890	76	6	R
Quantitative Reasoning	894	81	7	Q
Mathematics Achievement	883	61	6	M

LEGEND: V = Verbal Reasoning R = Reading Comprehension Q = Quantitative Reasoning M = Mathematics Achievement

ANALYSIS

Section & Subsection	# of Questions	# Correct	Results for Each Question
Verbal Reasoning			
Synonyms	18	15	+++++++- ++++- ++- +
Single Word Response	17	16	+++++++++++- +++++
Quantitative Reasoning			
Word Problems	18	11	+++- - - +++- +++++- - -
Quantitative Comparisons	14	14	++++++++++++++
Reading Comprehension			
Main Idea	4	4	++++
Supporting Ideas	6	5	- +++++
Inference	6	5	+- ++++
Vocabulary	7	5	+++- +- +
Organization/Logic	4	4	++++
Tone/Style/Figurative Language	3	3	+++
Mathematics Achievement			
Whole Numbers	7	4	+- +++- -
Decimals, Percents, Fractions	9	5	++- - ++- - +
Algebraic Concepts	11	7	+++++- ++- - -
Geometry	4	2	+- +-
Measurement	5	4	++++-
Data Analysis and Probability	6	4	+++- +-

LEGEND: + = Correct   - = Incorrect   S = Skipped   N = Not Reached

The test was administered in the order reported in the analysis section; Verbal Reasoning, Quantitative Reasoning, Reading Comprehension, and Mathematics Achievement. Each section was divided into subsections, grouping similar types of questions. The Reading Comprehension subsection grouping does not represent the actual order of the test questions.

The above is a preliminary ISEE report. ERB reserves the right to amend this report before it is finalized. The report will be final no later than 20 business days. The final report will automatically be generated electronically.